HOW TO

BREAK UP

WITH YOUR

PHONE

HOW TO
BREAK UP
WITH YOUR
PHONE

CATHERINE PRICE

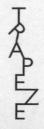

For Clara

Your life is what you pay attention to

First published in Great Britain in 2018 by Trapeze,
an imprint of The Orion Publishing Group Ltd
Carmelite House, 50 Victoria Embankment,
London EC4Y 0DZ

An Hachette UK company

10 9 8

A CIP catalogue record for this book is
available from the British Library.

ISBN (Hardback): 978 1 409 17626 8
ISBN (eBook): 978 1 409 17627 5

Design by Lizzie Allen

Printed and bound by CPI Group (UK) Ltd,
Croydon, CR0 4YY

MIX
Paper from
responsible sources
FSC® C104740

www.orionbooks.co.uk

CONTENTS

AN OPEN LETTER TO MY PHONE

Dear Phone,

I still remember the first time we met. You were an expensive new gadget available only through AT&T; I was a person who could recite her best friends' phone numbers from memory. When you were launched, I'll admit that your touch screen caught my eye. But I was too busy trying to type a text message on my flip phone to start something new.

Then I held you in my hand, and things started moving fast. It wasn't long before we were doing everything together: taking walks, having lunch with friends, going on vacations. At first it seemed strange that you wanted to come with me to the bathroom – but today it's just another formerly private moment for us to share.

We're inseparable now, you and I. You're the last thing I touch before I go to bed and the first thing I reach for in the morning. You remember my doctors' appointments, my shopping lists, and my anniversary. You provide GIFs and festive emoji that I can send to friends on their birthdays, so that rather than feeling hurt that I'm texting instead of calling, they think, "Ooh, animated balloons!" You make it possible for my avoidance strategies to be construed as thoughtfulness, and for this I am grateful.

Phone, you are amazing. I mean that literally: not only do you allow me to travel across time and space, but I am amazed by how many nights I've stayed up three hours past my bedtime staring at your screen. I can't count the times where we've gone to bed together and I've had to pinch myself to see if I'm dreaming – and believe me, I want to be dreaming, because ever since we met, something seems to be messing with my sleep. I cannot believe all of the gifts you've given me, even though many of those gifts are technically things that I bought for myself online while you and I were "relaxing" in a bath.

Thanks to you, I never need to worry about being alone. Any time I'm anxious or upset, you offer a game or newsfeed or viral panda video to distract me from my feelings. And how about boredom? Just a few years ago, I'd often find myself with no way to pass the time other than to daydream, or maybe think. There were even times when I'd get into the lift at the office and have nothing to look at but the other passengers. For six floors!

These days, I can't even remember the last time I was bored. Then again, I can't remember a lot of things. Like, for example, the last time my friends and I made it through a meal without anyone pulling out a phone. Or how it felt to be able to read an entire magazine article in one sitting. Or what I said in the paragraph above this one. Or whose text I was looking at right before I walked into that pole.

Or whatever. My point is, I feel like I can't live without you.

And that's why it's so hard for me to tell you that we need to break up.

INTRODUCTION

Let's get something clear from the start: the point of this book is not to get you to throw your phone under a bus. Just as breaking up with a person doesn't mean that you're swearing off all human relationships, "breaking up" with your phone doesn't mean that you're trading in your touch screen for a rotary dial.

After all, there are lots of reasons for us to love our smartphones. They're cameras. They're DJs. They help us keep in touch with family and friends, and they know the answers to every piece of trivia we could ever think to ask. They tell us about the traffic and the weather; they store our calendars and our contact lists. Smartphones are amazing tools.

But something about smartphones also makes *us* act like tools. Most of us find it hard to get through a meal or a film or even a stoplight without pulling out our phones. On the rare occasions when we accidentally leave them at home or on our desk, we reach for them anyway, and feel anxious, again and again, each time we realise they're not there. If you're like most people, your phone is within arm's reach right this very second, and the mere mention of it is making you want to check something. Like the news. Or your texts. Or your email. Or the weather. Or, really, anything at all.

Go ahead and do it. And then come back to this page and notice how you feel. Are you calm? Focused? Present? Satisfied? Or are you feeling a bit scattered and uneasy, vaguely stressed without really knowing why?

Today, just over a decade since smartphones entered our lives, we're beginning to suspect that their impact on our lives might not be entirely good. We feel busy but ineffective. Connected but lonely. The same technology that gives us freedom can also act like a leash – and the more tethered we become, the more it raises the question of who's actually in control. The result is a paralysing tension: we love our phones, but we often hate the way they make us feel. And no one seems to know what to do about it.

The problem isn't smartphones themselves. The problem is our relationships with them. Smartphones have infiltrated our lives so quickly and so thoroughly that we have never stopped to think about what we actually want our relationships with them to look like – or what effects these relationships might be having on our lives.

We've never stopped to think about which features of our phones make us feel good, and which make us feel bad. We've never stopped to think about why smartphones are so hard to put down, or who might be benefiting when we pick them up. We've never stopped to think about what spending so many hours engaged with our devices might be doing to our brains, or whether a device billed as a way to connect us to other people might actually be driving us apart.

"Breaking up" with your phone means giving yourself a chance to stop and think.

It means noticing which parts of your relationship are working and which parts are not. It means setting boundaries between your online and offline lives. It means becoming conscious of how and why you use your phone – and recognising that your phone is manipulating how and why you use it. It means undoing the effects that your phone has had on your brain. It means prioritising real-life relationships over those that take place on screens.

Breaking up with your phone means giving yourself the space, freedom, and tools necessary to create a new, long-term relationship with it, one that keeps what you love about your phone and gets rid of what you don't. A relationship, in other words, that makes you feel healthy and happy – and over which you have control.

IF YOU'RE CURIOUS ABOUT THE status of your relationship with your smartphone, try taking the Smartphone Compulsion Test, developed by Dr. David Greenfield, founder of the Center for Internet and Technology Addiction and psychiatry professor at the University of Connecticut School of Medicine. Just circle the questions that apply to you.

1. Do you find yourself spending more time on your mobile or smartphone than you realise?

2. Do you find yourself mindlessly passing time on a regular basis by staring at your mobile or smartphone?

3. Do you seem to lose track of time when on your mobile or smartphone?

4. Do you find yourself spending more time texting, tweeting, or emailing as opposed to talking to people in person?

5. Has the amount of time you spend on your mobile or smartphone been increasing?

6. Do you wish you could be a little less involved with your phone?

7. Do you sleep with your mobile or smartphone (turned on) under your pillow or next to your bed regularly?

8. Do you find yourself viewing and answering texts, tweets, and emails at all hours of the day and night – even if it means interrupting other things you are doing?

9. Do you text, email, tweet, Snapchat, Facebook message, or surf while driving or doing other similar activities that require your focused attention and concentration?

10. Do you feel your use of your mobile or smartphone decreases your productivity at times?

11. Do you feel reluctant to be without your mobile or smartphone, even for a short time?

12. Do you feel ill at ease or uncomfortable when you accidentally leave your smartphone in the car or at home, have no service, or have a broken phone?

13. When you eat meals, is your mobile or smartphone always part of the table place setting?

14. When your mobile or smartphone rings, beeps, or buzzes, do you feel an intense urge to check for texts, tweets, emails, updates, and so on?

15. Do you find yourself mindlessly checking your mobile or smartphone many times a day, even when you know it is unlikely there is anything new or important to see?

Here's how Greenfield interprets people's scores:

1–2: Your behaviour is normal but that doesn't mean you should live on your smartphone.

3–4: Your behaviour is leaning toward problematic or compulsive use.

5 or above: It is likely that you may have a problematic or compulsive smartphone use pattern.

8 or higher: If your score is higher than 8, you might consider seeing a psychologist, psychiatrist, or psycho-therapist who specialises in behavioural addictions for a consultation.

If you are like most people, you have just discovered that you qualify for a psychiatric evaluation. I mean, come on. The only way to score below 5 on this test is to not have a smartphone.

But the fact that these behaviours and feelings are so universal does not mean that they are harmless or that this test is too dramatic. Instead, it's an indication that the problem may be bigger than we think. To prove it, try this game: the next time you're in public, take a second to notice how many of the people around you – including children – are staring at their phones. Then imagine that instead of looking at their smartphones, those same people were shooting up. Would the fact that half the people around you were doing so make it seem normal or okay?

I'm not suggesting that smartphones are actually as addictive as intravenous drugs. But I do think that we're kidding ourselves if we don't believe we have a problem.

Consider the following:

- UK adults check their phones about 33 times per day. Young people aged between 16 and 19 average 90 checks per day.

- On average, Britons spend more than 2 hours a day on their phones. That amounts to about 14 hours a week, 60 hours a month, or 30 full days a year.

- More than a third of UK adults look at their phones within five minutes of waking and over half do so within fifteen minutes.

- 38 per cent of adults check their phones after they have gone to sleep. Among teenagers, this figure rises to 66 per cent, and over a quarter respond to their messages during the night.

- We're using our phones so much that we're giving ourselves repetitive strain injuries such as "texting thumb", "text neck", and "mobile phone elbow".

- 91 per cent of the 41 million 16-75 year olds who have a smartphone in the UK use their device every day.

- 62 per cent of UK consumers agree with this statement: "I can't imagine my life without my mobile phone".

- Studies suggest that up to 62 per cent of women and 48 per cent of men have checked their phone during sex.

  Yes, sex.

Strangely, while many people agree that taking a break from their phones (often called "unplugging" or taking a "digital detox") would be good for their mental health, very few people actually do it.

As a health and science journalist, I find this discrepancy fascinating. But my interest is personal, too. I have spent more than fifteen years writing books and articles about subjects ranging from diabetes, nutritional chemistry, and endocrinology to mindfulness, positive psychology, and meditation. Other than a brief stint as a Latin and maths teacher, I've always been my own boss – and as anyone who's started their own business knows, surviving as a freelancer requires a lot of self-discipline and focus. (I spent three years writing a history of vitamins, for goodness' sake.) You'd think that by now my time-management skills must be pretty well honed.

But over the past few years, they've actually become worse. My attention span is shorter. My memory seems weaker. My focus flickers. Sure, some of this might be due to natural age-related changes in my brain. The more I thought about it, however, the more I began to suspect that there was an external factor at play – and that that factor was my phone.

In contrast to my adult life, my childhood was relatively screen-free. We had a television and I loved after-school cartoons, but I also spent a considerable number of weekend mornings lying in bed reading *Anne of Green Gables* and/or staring blankly at the ceiling. I entered secondary school around the same time that my family got its first dial-up modem, and quickly became enthralled by

America Online – or, to be more specific, "teen chat" rooms, where I delighted in flirting with faceless strangers and correcting people's grammar for hours at a time. I graduated from college just as first-generation mobile phones (that is, "dumbphones") were becoming widespread. I'm part of the generation, in other words, that came of age along with the internet: I'm old enough to remember the world before it, but young enough that I can't imagine life without it.

I got my first smartphone in 2010, and before long I was carrying it with me everywhere I went and picking it up constantly – sometimes just for seconds, and sometimes for hours at a time. In retrospect, other things were also happening: I was reading fewer books, for example, and spending less time with friends and on hobbies, such as playing music, that I knew brought me joy. My shortened attention span was making it harder for me to be present in those other activities even when I did do them. But at the time, it didn't occur to me that these things might be connected.

Just as it can take a long time to realise that a romantic relationship is unhealthy, it took me a long time to realise that something felt off about my interactions with my phone. I began to notice that I often picked up my phone "just to check", only to resurface an hour later wondering where the time had gone. I'd respond to a text and then get caught in a thirty-minute back-and-forth that felt more demanding than an in-person conversation and yet left me feeling less fulfilled. I'd open an app with a sense of anticipation, and then be disappointed when it didn't provide the satisfaction that I sought.

There wasn't anything inherently wrong about the

things I was doing; what made me feel weird was how often I initiated them without thinking, how many real-life experiences they were supplanting, and how crappy they made me feel. I reached for my phone to soothe myself, but I often crossed the line from feeling soothed to going numb.

I realised that I had developed a physical tic where any time I hit "Save" on the document I was working on, I automatically reached for my phone to check my email. Any time I had to wait for anything – a friend, a doctor, a lift – my phone appeared in my hand. I found myself glancing at my phone in the middle of conversations (a habit that's so common that it's coined a neologism: *phubbing*, short for *phone snubbing*), conveniently forgetting how annoyed I felt when other people phubbed me. I was gripped by a constant compulsion to pick up my phone, presumably so that I didn't miss something important. But when I evaluated what I was doing, *important* was pretty much the last word that came to mind.

What's more, far from relieving my anxiety, checking my phone nearly always contributed to it. I'd look at it for a second before bed, notice a stressful email in my inbox, and then lie awake for an hour worrying about something that could easily have waited until morning. I'd reach for it to give myself a break, and then end up feeling exhausted and wired. I claimed not to have enough time to pursue interests outside of work, but was that true?

I worried that my increasing tendency to app-source so many aspects of my life – from getting directions to deciding where to eat – might be causing the smartphone version of the expression *When all you have is a hammer, every problem looks like a nail*: the more I used my phone to navigate my life, the less capable I felt of navigating life without my phone.

My research suggested that I was far from alone in my concerns. So I decided to turn my personal curiosity into a professional project. I wanted to understand the mental, social, and physical effects that my phone time was having on me. I wanted to know whether my smartphone could be making me dumb.

MY FIRST ATTEMPTS AT INVESTIGATION didn't get very far. I was too distractible. In fact, the earliest journal entry I wrote about smartphones reads like the diary of someone with an attention disorder. I jump from a rant against people who cross the street while texting to a description of an app that discourages phone use by entrusting you with the care of a digital forest to the admission that, in the midst of scribbling these disjointed thoughts, I had gone online and purchased three sports bras.

Once I'd finally managed to corral my concentration, I found evidence that there might indeed be a connection between my diminished attention span and the time I was spending on my smartphone and other internet-connected wireless mobile devices (which some researchers quasi-jokingly refer to as WMDs).* While research on these devices is in its early stages (unsurprising, given that they've barely been around for ten years), what is known so far suggests that spending extended time on them has the power to change both the structure and the function of our brains – including our abilities to form new memories, think deeply, focus, and absorb and remember what we read. Multiple studies have associated the heavy use of smartphones (especially when used for social media) with negative effects on neuroticism, self-esteem, impulsivity, empathy, self-identity, and self-image, as well as with sleep problems, anxiety, stress, and depression.

Speaking of things that are depressing, many researchers are concluding that smartphones are having a huge impact on the way we (especially teenagers) are interacting – or, rather, *not* interacting – with other real live human beings. The psychological effects of transferring our social interactions onto screens are so severe that Jean Twenge, author of a book called *iGen* (short for *iGeneration* – people who have grown up with smartphones), concludes that "it's not an exaggeration to describe iGen as being on the brink of the worst mental-health crisis in decades". According to Twenge, who has been researching generational differences for twenty-five years (and claims to have never seen so many dramatic changes occur so rapidly), "much of this deterioration can be traced to their phones".

I learned about the history of written language, and how the act of reading itself – as in books, not "listicles" – can change the brain in ways that encourage deep thought. I looked into what's known about how the way information is presented on the internet threatens our attention

----

* A more accurate title for this book might actually be *How to Break Up with Your Wireless Mobile Device*, given that tablets can be similarly problematic, and it won't be long before smartphones are supplanted by something else. I'm going to stick with the current title, but please feel free to swap out phone for whatever WMD you're currently in a relationship with.

spans and memories, and how smartphones in particular have been deliberately designed to be difficult to put down (and whom this benefits). I read about habits and addictions, neuroplasticity, and how smartphones are causing otherwise mentally healthy people to show signs of psychiatric problems such as narcissism, obsessive-compulsive disorder (OCD), and attention deficit hyperactivity disorder (ADHD).

I also looked back at interviews I'd conducted over the many years I've spent writing articles about mental and physical health. The deeper I got, the more I began to see my phone as my partner in a dysfunctional relationship: someone (or, rather, some*thing*) with the power both to make me feel bad about myself and to keep me coming back for more. And the more I read, the more I became convinced that our attachment to our devices is not a trivial issue. It is a real problem – I'd go so far as to say that it's a societal addiction – and we need to do something about it.

No matter how hard I looked, however, I couldn't find the primary thing I sought: a solution. Some of the books and articles offered tips and tricks for how to reduce phone time through some combination of restrictions and restraint. But these felt like superficial treatments for a much more complicated problem.

What I realised was that we reach for our phones for many reasons, some of which are purely practical, some of which are subconscious, and some of which are surprisingly emotionally deep. Simply telling ourselves to spend less time on our phones is the equivalent of telling ourselves to stop being attracted to people who are bad for us: it's easier said than done, and is probably going to require a good therapist – or at the very least, an extremely well-considered plan.

But such a plan didn't seem to exist. So I decided to create one.

MY FIRST STEP WAS A personal experiment: my husband and I decided to do a digital detox by taking a twenty-four-hour break from phones and all other internet-enabled devices. As we sat down for dinner one Friday night, I lit a candle, we gave our phones one final glance, and then we turned them off – all the way off – for the next twenty-four hours. We avoided our tablets and computers, too. From Friday to Saturday night, we completely disconnected ourselves from our screens.

It was an eye-opening experience, both in terms of how unusual it felt, and how it made us feel. At first we were constantly tempted to reach for our phones – which we convinced ourselves was out of concern that we would miss an important phone call or text but, if we were being honest, was actually a sign of dependency. But we resisted our urges and, when the time came for us to turn our phones back on, we were surprised by how reluctant we were to do so – and how quickly our attitudes had shifted. Instead of being stressful, the experience had felt restorative, so much so that we decided to do it again.

We called the ritual a "digital Sabbath", and by the second or third time we'd done it, we'd settled into a rhythm and worked out the kinks. Without our phones to distract us, time seemed to slow down. We went on walks. We read books. We talked more. I felt healthier and more grounded, as if I were getting back in touch with a part of myself that I hadn't even realised had gone missing. Interestingly, the effects of the Sabbath seemed to linger for several days afterward – a sort of digital hangover that actually felt *good*.

This made me want to make changes to my relationship with my phone during the rest of the week as well, to see if I could make these positive feelings more permanent. But how could I do this without going cold turkey? I didn't want my phone to control me, but I also knew I didn't want to give up my phone completely. That would mean throwing out the good with the bad.

Instead, I wanted balance. I wanted a new relationship with my phone, one in which I used my phone when it was helpful or fun, but didn't get sucked into spirals of mindless swiping. And in order to create a new relationship, I realised I needed to take a step back from the one I was currently in. I needed time. I needed space. I needed to break up with my phone.

WHEN I TOLD PEOPLE I was breaking up with my phone, they didn't ask me what I meant, or why I wanted to do it. Instead, they said the same thing, practically verbatim: "I need to do that, too."

I decided to enlist their help. I sent out an email recruiting volunteers, and soon had a list of nearly 150 guinea pigs, who ranged in age from twenty-one to seventy-three. They came from six countries and fifteen American states. There were teachers, lawyers, doctors, writers, marketers, publicists, homemakers, data scientists, computer programmers, editors, professional investors, nonprofit directors, and self-employed business owners – including a jewellery maker, a graphic designer, a music teacher, a personal chef, and an interior designer.

I created readings and assignments based on my research on mindfulness, habits, choice architecture, distraction, focus, attention, meditation, product design, behavioural addictions, neuroplasticity, psychology, sociology, and the history of disruptive technologies. After trying my ideas on myself, I sent them to my guinea pigs and asked for feedback and suggestions, which I then incorporated into the plan.

I was amazed by how candid people were in their responses, and how many common themes emerged. By the end of the group experiment, I'd come to three conclusions. The first was that this problem is widespread: many people worry that they're addicted to their phones. The second was that despite the claims of naysayers, we have the power to break this addiction. And the third was that breaking up with your phone doesn't just have the potential to change your relationship with your devices. It can also change your life.

We're never going to break up with our phones unless we think it's vitally important to do so. That's why the first half of this book, "The Wake-Up", is designed to freak you out. It's a synthesis of how and why our phones are designed to be hard to put down, and what effect spending so much time on them may be having on our relationships and our mental and physical health. In other words, it's the part of the break up when your best friend pulls you aside at a bar one night and starts to itemise all the ways that your boyfriend or girlfriend is making you miserable, and at first you're like, "Leave me alone! It's my life!" but by the end of the conversation you realise that they're right and then panic because you don't know what to do.

The second half of the book, "The Break-up," tells you what to do. It's a 30-day plan designed to help you establish a new, healthier relationship with your phone. Don't worry – except for one twenty-four-hour period, I'm not going to ask you to be separated from your phone. Instead, I've provided a series of exercises meant to smoothly guide you through the process of creating a new, personalised relationship that is both sustainable and makes you feel good.

I've also included lots of quotations from people who've already gone through the process as inspiration. (I've changed some of the names to protect their privacy.)

As I write this, it occurs to me that there are two groups of people who will be reading this book: people who bought it for themselves, and people who had it given to them by a concerned friend/parent/relative/roommate/spouse and may not be entirely "appreciative" of this "gift".

Second group, I'm sorry: it's never fun to have someone tell you they think you have a problem. But allow me to let you in on a secret: *whoever gave you this book is probably addicted to their phone, too.* And even if they aren't too bad themselves, you certainly know other people who might benefit from re-evaluating their relationship with their phones. So I encourage you to see if any of the book's ideas resonate with you. Then, when you're done, give it back to the person who gave it to you – maybe with a handwritten note that says, "Your turn".

Regardless of who you are or why you're doing this, breaking up with your phone definitely has its challenges. It requires self-reflection and the determination to wrest your life back from a device that has been specifically designed to make it difficult to do so.

But as I and the other people who have broken up with their phones can attest, it is more than worth it. Not only will breaking up with your phone help you establish a healthier relationship with technology, but it will also have effects in areas of your life that you never imagined your phone could touch. The more you notice your interactions with your phone, the more aware you'll become of the world *off* your phone – and of how much of it you've been missing. Breaking up with your phone will allow you to reconnect with a part of you that knows that life doesn't happen on a screen. And the faster you can get in touch with it, the better.

*Every once in a while, a
revolutionary product comes
along that changes everything.*

—Steve Jobs, introducing the first iPhone in 2007

part i

THE

WAKE-

UP

1

OUR PHONES
ARE DESIGNED TO
ADDICT US

Whenever you check for a new post on Instagram
or whenever you go on the *New York Times* to see if
there's a new thing, it's not even about the content.
It's just about seeing a new thing.
You get addicted to that feeling.

—Aziz Ansari

IT'S TEMPTING TO THINK OF smartphones as just one
more technology in a long list of technologies that have
freaked people out. Telegraphs, telephones, radios, movies,
television, video games, even books – all caused panic when
they were first introduced, and all have turned out to be less
harmful than people feared.

But, while we shouldn't be alarmist, Steve Jobs was right: smartphones really are different. They're different in a lot of good ways, obviously. But smartphones also talk back at us. They nag us. They disturb us when we're working. They demand our attention and reward us when we give it to them. Smartphones engage in disruptive behaviours that have traditionally been performed only by extremely annoying people. What's more, they give us access to the entire internet. And, unlike previous technologies, we keep them near us at all times.

Smartphones are also one of the first popular technologies to be specifically engineered to get us to spend time on them. In the words of Tristan Harris, a former Google product manager who's now working to raise awareness about how our devices are designed to manipulate us, "Your telephone in the 1970s didn't have a thousand engineers on the other side of the telephone who were redesigning it . . . to be more and more persuasive."

Perhaps this is part of the reason that Jobs – the man who introduced the iPhone – restricted his own children's access to his company's products. "They haven't used it," he said, when *New York Times* technology reporter Nick Bilton asked him if his children liked the iPad. "We limit how much technology our kids use at home."

The same is true of Microsoft founder Bill Gates and his wife, Melinda, who didn't give their kids phones until they were fourteen. Indeed, according to Bilton, many technology chief executives and venture capitalists "strictly limit their children's screen time" – which he took to suggest that "these tech C.E.O.s seem to know something that the rest of us don't".

An increasing number of mental health experts are concluding that this "something" is the risk of addiction. This might seem like a dramatic term to use, given that we're talking about a device, not a drug. But not all addictions are to drugs or alcohol – we can get addicted to behaviours, too, such as gambling or even exercise. And addictions exist on a spectrum; it's possible to be addicted to something without it destroying your life.

Addiction can be defined as continuing to seek out something (for example, drugs or gambling), despite negative consequences. In his book *The Brain That Changes Itself*, Canadian psychiatrist Norman Doidge explains the general characteristics of addiction like this: "Addicts show a loss of control of the activity, compulsively seek it out despite negative consequences, develop tolerance so that they need higher and higher levels of stimulation for satisfaction, and experience withdrawal if they can't consummate the addictive act."

That certainly would seem to describe the way many of us feel about our smartphones. And indeed, many technology companies themselves seem comfortable with the term (case in point, a 2015 Consumer Insights report from Microsoft Canada that featured a full-page infographic with the heading "Addictive Technology Behaviors Are Evident, Particularly for Younger Canadians"). But if you don't like the word *addiction*, that's fine – you can call it whatever you want. The point is that many of the same feel-good brain chemicals and reward loops that drive addictions are also released and activated when we check our phones.

The point is also that revolutionary technologies don't just "come along," as Jobs put it; they're designed. Not only are phone and app companies aware of their products' neurological effects, but they pack their products with features that will trigger them – with the explicit goal of getting us to spend as much time and attention as possible on our devices. In industry terms, this is called "user engagement". Why do companies care so much about engagement? Because, as we'll talk about in more detail in a bit, it's how they make money.

This is not to suggest that tech companies are out to deliberately hurt people (on the contrary, many of the people who work at them affirmatively want to make the world better), and it's important to note that the features that make smartphones potentially problematic are the same features that make them easy to use and fun. Take away the possibility of getting hooked, and you'd take away all the reasons we like smartphones to begin with.

Nonetheless, the fact that so many tech executives limit their own kids' exposure suggests that they don't think the benefits always outweigh the risks – to the point that they feel the need to protect their families from the devices that they create. It's the Silicon Valley version of the drug dealer's adage: "Never get high on your own supply."

2

PUTTING
THE *DOPE* IN
DOPAMINE

Just as drugs have become more powerful over time, so has the thrill of behavioural feedback. Product designers are smarter than ever. They know how to push our buttons and how to encourage us to use their products not just once but over and over.

—Adam Alter, *Irresistible: The Rise of Addictive Technology and the Business of Keeping Us Hooked*

IN ORDER TO MAXIMISE THE amount of time we spend on our devices, designers manipulate our brain chemistry in ways that are known to trigger addictive behaviours.

Most of these techniques involve a brain chemical called dopamine. Dopamine has many roles, but for our purposes the most important thing to know is that, by activating pleasure-related receptors in our brains, it teaches us to associate certain behaviours with rewards (think of a rat that gets a pellet every time it presses a lever). Dopamine makes us feel excited – and we like feeling excited. Any experience that triggers the release of dopamine is therefore something that we'll want to experience again.

But that's not all. If an experience consistently triggers the release of dopamine, our brains remember the cause and effect. Eventually, they will release dopamine any time they're *reminded* of the experience. They'll release it, in other words, in anticipation.

The ability to anticipate satisfaction is essential for our survival – it motivates us to seek out food, for example. But it also causes cravings and, in more extreme cases, addictions. If your brain learns that checking your phone usually results in a reward, it won't take long before your brain releases dopamine any time it's reminded of your phone. You'll start to crave it. (Ever notice how seeing someone else check their phone can make you want to check yours?)

Interestingly, these "rewards" can be positive *or* negative. Sometimes we reach for our phones out of hope/ anticipation that there'll be something good waiting for us. But just as often, we reach for our phones to help us avoid something unpleasant, such as boredom or anxiety. It doesn't matter. Once our brains have learned to associate checking our phones with getting a reward, we are going to really, really, really want to check our phones. We become like the lab rats, constantly pressing the lever to get food.

Thankfully, food cravings naturally subside when our stomachs feel full (otherwise our stomachs might explode).

But phones and most apps are deliberately designed without "stopping cues" to alert us when we've had enough – which is why it's so easy to accidentally binge. On a certain level, we know that what we're doing is making us feel gross. But instead of stopping, our brains decide the solution is to seek out more dopamine. We check our phones again. And again. And again.

When this happens, we tend to blame our binges on a lack of willpower – another way of saying that we blame ourselves. What we don't realise is that technology designers deliberately manipulate our dopamine responses to make it extremely difficult for us to stop using their products. Known as "brain hacking", this is essentially behavioural design based on brain chemistry – and once you know how to recognise its signs, you'll see it all over your phone.

In 2017, *60 Minutes* aired a fascinating interview between Anderson Cooper and Ramsay Brown, founder of a start-up called Dopamine Labs that creates brain-hacking code for app companies. The goal is to keep people glued to an app by figuring out exactly when the app should do something to "make you feel a little extra awesome," explained Brown, who has a background in neuroscience (and who, for the record, comes across as a thoughtful and un-evil kind of guy).

Brown offered the example of Instagram, which he says has created code that deliberately holds back on showing users new "likes" so that it can deliver a bunch of them in a sudden rush at the most effective moment possible – meaning the moment at which seeing new likes will discourage you from closing the app. And when he says "you", Brown means *you*.

As he explained to Anderson Cooper, "There's an algorithm somewhere that predicted, hey, for this user right now who is experimental subject 79B3 in experiment 231, we think we can see an improvement in his behaviour if you give it to him in this burst instead of that burst.... You're part of a set of controlled experiments that are happening in real time across you and millions of other people."

"We're guinea pigs?" asked Cooper.

"You're guinea pigs," said Brown. "You're guinea pigs in the box pushing the button and sometimes getting the likes. And they're doing this to keep you in there."

Interestingly, Brown – who is one of the few technology insiders who agreed to speak with *60 Minutes* on the record – also created an app called Space that was meant to encourage people to spend *less* time on their phones by creating a twelve-second delay before social media apps would open. Brown called this a "moment of Zen"; the point was to give people a chance to change their minds.

But the App Store initially refused to sell Space. "They rejected it from the App Store because they told us any app that would encourage people to use other apps or their iPhones less was unacceptable for distribution in the App Store," said Brown. "They did not want us to give out this thing that was gonna make people less stuck on their phones."*

---

* *60 Minutes* later reported that "a few days after our story first aired, Apple called to tell us it had a change of heart and made 'Space' available in its App Store."

3

THE TRICKS OF
THE TRADE

Never before in history have the decisions of a
handful of designers (mostly men, white, living in San
Francisco, aged 25–35) working at three companies
had so much impact on how millions of people
around the world spend their attention.

—Tristan Harris, ex–Google employee
and design ethicist

THE BETTER WE UNDERSTAND OUR own dopamine responses, the better equipped we'll be to recognise brain
hacks when we see them. So let's take a phone's-eye look at
some of our psychological quirks – and how they're being
used to manipulate us.

WE ARE NOVELTY JUNKIES

You know that heady feeling you get early on in a romantic relationship where you crave spending time with the person? That's the work of dopamine, too – it's released any time we experience something new.

But once the novelty wears off, less dopamine is released. This is the post-honeymoon phase of human relationships where someone often gets dumped. But we'll never get to the point of even *considering* dumping our smartphones, because phones (and apps) are designed to provide us with constant novelty – and as a result, constant hits of dopamine.

Feeling bored or anxious? Check your email. Nothing there? Check social media. Not satisfied? Check a different social media account. And then maybe another one. Like a couple of posts. Follow some new people. Check to see if those people followed you back. Maybe go look at your email again, just in case. It's easy to spend hours on your phone without using the same app twice – or staying focused for more than a few seconds at a time.

It's worth pointing out that dopamine-induced excitement is not the same thing as actual happiness. But try telling that to our brains.

WE ARE TODDLERS

Anyone who's spent time with a two-year-old knows that toddlers are fascinated by cause and effect. Flip a switch on the wall, and a light goes on. Press a button and a doorbell rings. Express even the slightest interest in an electrical outlet and an adult will come running.

It's a trait we never outgrow: no matter what age we are, we really love getting reactions to things that we do. In psychology, these reactions are called "reinforcements", and the more reinforcements we get when we do something, the more likely we are to do it again. (Oddly, the reaction doesn't have to be positive. You might think that scolding a toddler for putting playdough in her mouth might discourage her from doing it again, but trust me: it does not.)

Our phones are packed with subtle positive reinforcements that trigger dopamine spritzes that keep us coming back for more. Touch a link, and a webpage appears. Send a text message and you'll hear a satisfying "whoosh". Cumulatively, these reinforcements give us a pleasant feeling of control – which in turn makes us want to constantly be on our phones.

WE FIND INCONSISTENCY IRRESISTIBLE

You'd think that the best way to get us to check our phones obsessively would be to make sure that there was *always* something good waiting for us.

But what really gets us hooked isn't consistency; it's unpredictability. It's knowing that something *could* happen – but not knowing when or if that something will occur.

Psychologists refer to unpredictable rewards as "intermittent reinforcements." I call them "the reason we date jerks." Regardless of what term you use, this unpredictability is incorporated into nearly every app on our phones.

When we check our phones, we occasionally find something satisfying – a complimentary email, a text from a crush, an interesting piece of news. The resulting burst of dopamine makes us begin to associate the act of checking our phones with the receipt of a reward. Similarly, there are times when checking your phone out of anxiety really does leave you feeling soothed.

Once that link has been established, it doesn't matter if we're rewarded only one time out of every fifty. Thanks to dopamine, our brains remember that one time. And instead of dissuading us, the fact that we can't predict which of our fifty checks is going to be rewarding makes us check our phones even more.

Want to know another device that uses intermittent rewards to drive compulsive behaviour? Slot machines.

In fact, the similarities between the two devices are so powerful that Harris frequently compares smartphones to slot machines that we keep in our pockets.

"When we pull our phone out of our pocket, we're playing a slot machine to see what notifications we got," he explained in an article titled "How Technology Is Hijacking Your Mind".

"When we swipe down our finger to scroll the Instagram feed, we're playing a slot machine to see what photo comes next. When we swipe faces left/right on dating apps, we're playing a slot machine to see if we got a match."

Harris's observations are particularly disturbing when you realise that slot machines, which are specifically designed to deliver rewards in a way that drives compulsive behaviour, are one of the most addictive devices ever to have been invented.

WE HATE FEELING ANXIOUS

Anxiety is evolutionarily important because it's very motivating (a lion who's anxious about food is more likely to survive than a lion who's chilling out). But it is also easy to trigger, and it can turn us into stress cases, especially when it can't be resolved.

According to Larry Rosen, a psychologist at California State University, Dominquez Hills, our phones deliberately incite anxiety by providing new information and emotional triggers every time we pick them up. This makes us worry that any time we put them down, even for a second, we might miss something.

The non-technical term for this anxiety is FOMO: fear of missing out (not to be confused with its underappreciated counterpart, JOMO: the *joy* of missing out). Human beings have always suffered from FOMO. But we were protected from developing a full-blown infection by the fact that, until smartphones, there was no easy way to find out about all the things we were missing out on. Once you'd left your home (and your landline) to go to one party, you had no way of knowing that another party going on at the same time might be more fun. For better or for worse, you were just at the party.

Not only do smartphones make it easy to find out about the things we're missing, but also – through notifications – they spray FOMO at us like a sneeze. We become convinced that the only way to protect ourselves is to constantly check our phones to make sure that we're not missing something. But instead of helping alleviate our phone-induced FOMO, this actually increases it, to the point where our adrenal glands release a squirt of cortisol – a stress hormone that plays a large role in fight-or-flight responses – every time we put down our phones. Cortisol makes us feel anxious. We don't like to feel anxious. So, in order to relieve our anxiety, we reach for our phones. We feel better for a moment; we put them down – and we feel anxious again. Infected by FOMO, we keep checking and touching and swiping and scrolling, trying to relieve our anxiety by doing something that, by reinforcing our habit loop, actually only increases it.

WE WANT TO BE LOVED

Human beings are social creatures, and we desperately want to feel like we belong.

It wasn't so long ago that this affirmation (or rejection) came from real live people – as happened to me in middle school when a group of my so-called friends rated our classmates' popularity on a scale of one to ten, and decided that I was a negative three.

For the record, a scale of one to ten does not include negative numbers. But the bigger point is that whereas my verdict was delivered in person and relatively privately, today it would have been posted online for everyone to see – and to vote on. Whether it's ratings on Uber or "likes" on social media, many of today's most popular apps actively encourage users to judge one another.

Those features aren't there by accident. Designers know that humans have an intrinsic desire for affirmation, and that the more ways there are for us to be judged, the more compulsively we'll monitor our score. In *Irresistible*, Adam

Alter describes the launch of the "Like" button on Facebook as having had a psychological effect that was "hard to exaggerate." As he puts it, "A post with zero likes wasn't just privately painful, but also a kind of public condemnation".

The fact that these judgments matter to us is just as questionable as why I still remember the popularity scale incident more than twenty-five years later. But there's no question that they do.

What's particularly weird is that we don't just *care* about other people's judgments; we *ask* for them. We post photos and comments to show others that we're lovable, that we're popular and, on a more existential level, that we matter, and then we check our phones obsessively to see if other people – or at least their online profiles – agree. (And even though we know that we're curating our own feeds to make our lives look as exciting and fun as possible, we forget that everyone else is doing the same thing.)

Put this all together, and it makes sense that spending a lot of time on social media could be associated with depression and lower self-esteem. What doesn't make sense is that we are deliberately choosing to relive the worst parts of secondary school.

WE ARE LAZY

There's a reason that platforms like YouTube and Netflix are designed to automatically play the next video or episode in your (or, rather, their) queue: it's harder to swim against the current than it is to float downstream. If the next episode of the show you're watching automatically starts playing five seconds after the previous one ends, you're less likely to stop watching. (Some platforms allow you to disable this feature. Try it, and see if it makes a difference to how many videos you watch.)

WE LIKE BEING PRECIOUS SNOWFLAKES

Humans love feeling like we're special, which is why designers provide so many ways for us to personalise our phones. We can display personal photos on our home and lock screens. We can assign our favourite songs as ringtones. We can hand-select the types of news articles that appear in our feeds.

These features make our phones more useful and fun. But the more our phones feel like reflections of ourselves (and our specialness), the more time we're going to want to spend on them. And if you take a critical look at your phone's personalisation settings – as in, what settings you have control over versus what settings you don't – you'll notice that we have lots of control over features that make us more likely to spend time on our phones, and very little control over those that don't.

For example, I *do* have the option to change the voice of my phone's virtual assistant from an American woman's to a British man's – and to ask that British man to tell me jokes. ("The past, present, and future walk into a bar. It was tense.")

But it has taken years (and at least one lawsuit) for phone makers to even begin to give us the ability to set auto-responses for text messages – hardly a revolutionary idea, given how long we've been able to set up vacation responses for email. In addition to making it easier to take a break from your phone, the option to auto-respond to text messages could save lives by eliminating one reason – namely, the fear of leaving someone hanging – that so many people text and drive.

Indeed, the more you think about this, the more likely you are to come to the same conclusion as Tristan Harris. "The closer we pay attention to the options we're given," he writes, "the more we'll notice when they don't actually align with our true needs."

WE SELF-MEDICATE

As we've talked about, the flip side of wanting to feel plea-sure is the desire to avoid feeling bad – ideally with as little effort as possible. That's why, instead of getting to the root of our negative feelings, we turn to alcohol or drugs ... or our phones.

In a 2017 article in the *New York Times,* Matt Richtel reported that there's been a decade-long trend toward less alcohol and drug use among American teenagers. Great news – unless kids are just replacing one possible addiction with another. The title of the article was "Are Teenagers Replacing Drugs with Smartphones?" and the conclusion among most of the experts quoted was that the answer is likely yes.

"I see her at this point and time as not being a person who is controlled in any way by smoking pot," one school psychologist was quoted saying about his own daughter. "[But] her phone is something she sleeps with."

WE FEAR OUR OWN MINDS

If our smartphones excel at one thing, it's making sure we never, ever have to be alone with ourselves.

And thank goodness. In 2014, researchers from the University of Virginia and Harvard University published the results of a two-part study in *Science* that demonstrated the lengths we'll go to avoid our own minds.

In the first experiment, volunteers received a mild electric shock, and then were asked whether the experience was unpleasant enough that they would pay to avoid being shocked again.

The researchers took the forty-two people who'd said that they would pay to avoid another shock and left them alone in undecorated rooms, without access to the internet or any other form of distraction, and instructed them to entertain themselves with their thoughts for fifteen minutes. They also told the participants that, if they wanted, they could press a button and receive another electric shock – as in, the same shock they'd just said they'd pay to not have repeated.

You'd think that no one would have taken them up on the offer, right? Wrong. Out of the forty-two participants, eighteen chose to give themselves a shock during the fifteen-minute experiment. *Eighteen.* (And not just once. In what is undoubtedly my favorite detail of the study, one outlier shocked himself 190 times.)

"What is striking," wrote the authors, "is that simply being alone with their own thoughts for 15 minutes was apparently so aversive that it drove many participants to self-administer an electric shock that they had earlier said they would pay to avoid."

BEWARE OF GEEKS BEARING GIFTS

Put this all together, and our phones are like digital Trojan horses: innocuous-seeming accessories packed with manipulative tricks meant to get us to let down our guard. As soon as we do so, our attention is theirs for the taking. And as we'll see in a moment, it's a very valuable prize.

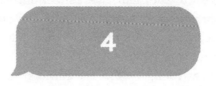

WHY SOCIAL
MEDIA SUCKS

Even more than it is in the advertising business,
Facebook is in the surveillance business. Facebook,
in fact, is the biggest surveillance-based enterprise in
the history of mankind. It knows far, far more about
you than the most intrusive government has ever
known about its citizens.

—John Lanchester

WHEN I ASK PEOPLE WHICH category of apps they find
the most problematic, social media is the most common
response. Like junk food, the content of these apps is hard
to stop consuming, even when you're aware that it's making
you feel sick.

It *should* make you feel sick. From its deliberately addictive design to its surveillance-based business model, social
media represents the epitome of "Trojan horse design": it's

meant to manipulate us into doing and sharing things we otherwise would not – often with negative effects on our mental health and society at large. And once you understand the forces behind social media, you may begin to think differently about many of the other apps and features on your phone, too.

Let's start with a question: have you ever wondered why social media apps are all free? It's not because their creators are driven by a philanthropic urge to help the world share selfies. It's because we are not actually the customers, and the social media platform itself is not the product.

Instead, the customers are advertisers. And the product being sold is our attention.

Think about it: the more attention we devote to Facebook or Twitter or a dating app or other social media, the more chances there are for the program to show us a sponsored post. And the more information we voluntarily post, the more personalised, attention-stealing, and profitable (for the social media company) the sponsored posts and ads will be.

In the words of Dopamine Labs founder Ramsay Brown, "You don't pay for Facebook. Advertisers pay for Facebook. You get to use it for free because your eyeballs are what's being sold there."

As we touched upon earlier, the prize these advertisers are after is "engagement", which is the metric by which companies evaluate the number of clicks, likes, shares, and comments associated with their content. Engagement is sometimes referred to as "the currency of the attention economy", and advertisers are willing to spend a lot of money for it. Global ad spending on social media in 2016 was $31 billion, almost double what it was just two years before.

In other words, every moment of attention we spend scrolling through social media is attention spent making money for someone else. The numbers are staggering: a *New York Times* analysis calculated that as of 2014, Facebook users were spending a collective 39,757 *years'* worth of attention on the site, *every single day*. It's attention that we didn't spend on our families, or our friends, or ourselves. And just like time, once we've spent attention, we can never get it back.

This is a really big deal, because our attention is the most valuable thing we have. We experience only what we pay attention to. We remember only what we pay attention to. When we decide what to pay attention to in the moment, we are making a broader decision about how we want to spend our lives.

To be clear, there is nothing wrong with spending your attention on social media (or on any other app). There is also nothing wrong with a designer trying to make an app that's fun, engaging, and profitable. But as users, we should be using our apps because we've made a conscious choice to do so – *not* because of manipulative psychological tricks that are meant to make money for someone else.

SOCIAL MEDIA KNOWS HOW TO STEAL OUR ATTENTION

Once you're aware of the motives behind social media platforms – namely, attention stealing and information gathering – you'll begin to notice how these motives are incorporated into their designs.

As we've discussed, "Like" buttons and comment features aren't just there to help us connect with other people; they're there because adding metrics to social interactions is a guaranteed way to keep us going back to see our "score."

HOW TO UNLIKE "LIKES"

If you find yourself obsessed with amassing likes, you may want to install a Facebook demetricator browser plug-in – it removes all the "scores" from Facebook so that instead of saying "57 people liked your post", it will simply say, "People like this". See if this makes a difference. Then ask yourself why Facebook itself doesn't provide this option.

Similarly, it would be easy for social media apps to be built with optional "stopping cues" to help us control our consumption. An app could give you the choice to see posts only from the last hour or day, or to set a limit for how much time you want to spend looking at your feed. But providing options like this might reduce "engagement". So instead, the feeds are deliberately designed to be endless. And even though we know that we will never "finish" our feeds, we keep scrolling, in pursuit of the dopamine hits that we get from every new post.

SOCIAL MEDIA IS
MAKING US DEPRESSED

Perhaps one of the most disturbing aspects of social media is the effects that it is having on our real-life relationships with other people – and, as a consequence, on our mental health.

Most people sign up for social media accounts out of a desire to feel connected – but numerous studies suggest that the more we use social media, the less happy we will be. In 2017, the *American Journal of Epidemiology* looked at the same group of people over time, hoping to determine whether social media use actually *caused* unhappiness, as opposed to simply appealing to people who were already unhappy. It concluded that there does indeed appear to be a causal relationship. As the authors described their results in the *Harvard Business Review*, "We found consistently that both liking others' content and clicking links significantly predicted a subsequent reduction in self-reported physical health, mental health, and life satisfaction."

In an article in *The Atlantic* titled, disturbingly, "Have Smartphones Destroyed a Generation", psychologist Jean Twenge presents compelling evidence that, as she puts it, "the arrival of the smartphone has radically changed every aspect of teenagers' lives, from the nature of their social interactions to their mental health". (While teenagers are extreme examples of this, I would argue that smartphones are doing the same to the rest of us, too.)

The article includes charts representing various trends in teenage behaviours from 1976 to 2016. From time spent hanging out with friends to the age of getting drivers' licences to dating to sleep to sex to (most strikingly) loneliness, the charts all have one thing in common: the slope of their lines changes dramatically after 2007, the year the first iPhone was released.

Look at this data together and it's hard not to come to the same conclusion as Twenge: "There is compelling evidence that the devices we've placed in young people's hands are having profound effects on their lives – and making them seriously unhappy". As she puts it, today's teens may be *physically* safer than their predecessors (less likely to drive drunk, for example). But that is likely because they are "on their phone, in their room, alone, and often distressed". Depression among teenagers is way up. Suicide rates are, too.

SOCIAL MEDIA IS BIG BROTHER

Imagine that someone knocked on your door and asked you to register the following information with the government: your full name, birth date, phone number, email address, physical address, education and work history, relationship status, names and photographs of all family members and friends, photographs and videos of yourself for as far back in time as possible, your political leanings, your travel history, your favourite books, your favourite music, and your favourite, well, *everything*. Would you?

On social media, we provide this information (and more) *voluntarily* – and with virtually no thought as to what the social media company might do with this information. As Antonio García Martínez, former product manager at Facebook, writes in his memoir, *Chaos Monkeys,* "The biggest thing going on in marketing right now, what is generating tens of billions of dollars in investment and endless scheming inside the bowels of Facebook, Google, Amazon, and Apple, is how to tie . . . different sets of [information] together, and who controls the links."

The amount of information that Facebook has about its users is truly shocking – García Martínez refers to Facebook as "the regulator of the biggest accumulation of personal data since DNA". What most of us don't realise is that Facebook doesn't just know everything you do and share on Facebook. Thanks to Facebook buttons and cookies (small files left behind on your computer that make it possible for companies to track your activities across sites), Facebook also knows many of the websites you've visited, apps you've used, and links you've clicked on. And thanks to partnerships with external data-collection companies such as Equifax, it knows countless details about your *offline* life, too, including (but not limited to!) your income and basically every purchase you've ever made with a card.

Finally, there's one more important reason to be aware of the motivations behind social media: the effects all this targeting and personalisation is having on society as a whole.

For as creepy as it might be to think of a company controlling this much data about such an enormous number of people, the only purpose, from Facebook's perspective, is to make Facebook money. On the positive side, this means that Facebook is very protective of its data because it's valuable. But the negative side is that Facebook does not have any intrinsic reason to care about whether the content that it's helping its advertisers share with us is factually accurate.

Instead, the goal is clicks. And when it comes to garnering clicks, the more sensational a post is, the better.

When you put this together with Facebook's ability to target ads (in this example, in the form of fake news stories) to the people who are the most likely to click on and share them, we end up in a situation where the stories that show up in my newsfeed might be completely different from those that show up in your newsfeed – and where none of them have been vetted to make sure they reflect any version of reality. The more this happens, the more we risk creating a society in which we no longer have a shared definition of the "truth".

THE TRUTH

ABOUT

MULTITASKING

The mind cannot have two thoughts at once.
See if you can think two thoughts at exactly
the same time. Well? Is it possible?

—Haemin Sunim, *The Things You Can See Only
When You Slow Down: How to Be Calm and
Mindful in a Fast-Paced World*

ONE OF THE MOST COMMON defences of phones is the idea that they're making us better at multitasking and, in so doing, more efficient.

Unfortunately, this isn't true. There's actually no such thing as multitasking (that is, simultaneously processing two or more attention-demanding tasks), because our brains can't do two cognitively demanding things at once.*

When we think we're multitasking, we're actually doing what researchers call "task-switching". Like cars making sharp turns, our brains need to slow down and switch gears every time we stop thinking about one thing and engage with another – a process that has been estimated to take twenty-five minutes every time you do it.

And I'm not just talking about multitasking at work (though most of us probably intuitively know that checking email when we're in the middle of a difficult task does not help our productivity). I also mean all the mini-multitasking that we engage in all day long: glancing at Twitter while we're also watching TV; looking at our email while we're on a call; even flipping quickly between apps as we wait in line to order lunch. You might think that you're able to simultaneously listen to your friend *and* respond to that text. But you can't.

In fact, we're often shifting the focus of our attention so rapidly that we never give ourselves enough time to get in gear to begin with. (When's the last time you spent twenty-five minutes just doing one thing?) Not only is this making us unproductive, but it's also affecting our ability to think and problem solve. It's also mentally exhausting.

And that's not all. In 2009, Stanford researchers led by Clifford Nass published a groundbreaking study in which they evaluated self-described heavy multitaskers' ability to perform a variety of tasks. The researchers hypothesised that

---

* Yes, we can do the dishes while we listen to the news. But that's not "multitasking" in the true sense of the word, because one activity is not cognitively demanding.

while multitasking might be draining at first, over time it must make people's brain better at *something*. They assumed that the heavy multitaskers in their study would be better than the controls at ignoring irrelevant information, switching efficiently between tasks, or organising their memories. But according to Nass, the researchers were wrong:

"We were absolutely shocked ... It turns out multi-taskers are terrible at every aspect of multitasking. They're terrible at ignoring irrelevant information; they're terrible at keeping information in their head nicely and neatly orga-nized; and they're terrible at switching from one task to another."

Perhaps worse? "One would think that if people were bad at multitasking, they would stop," said Nass. "However, when we talk with the multitaskers, they seem to think they're great at it and seem totally unfazed and totally able to do more and more and more."

Nass's conclusion? "We worry that [heavy multi-tasking] may be creating people who are unable to think well and clearly."

That itself is alarming – especially when you consider that multitasking (or at least *trying* to multitask) is exactly what our phones encourage us to do (not to mention the fact that Nass's research was published only two years after the first-generation iPhone was introduced). And it appears that, by weakening our attention spans and our memories, our phones are damaging our ability to *single*-task, too.

YOUR PHONE
IS CHANGING
YOUR BRAIN

Just as neurons that fire together wire together,
neurons that don't fire together don't wire together.
As the time we spend scanning Web pages crowds out
the time we spend reading books . . . the circuits that
support those old intellectual functions and pursuits
weaken and begin to break apart.

—Nicholas Carr, *The Shallows: What the Internet Is
Doing to Our Brains*

THE STRUCTURE OF OUR HEARTS and livers doesn't sub-
stantially change once those organs are formed. And until
surprisingly recently, scientists believed that the physical
structure of our brains – and the function of individual neurons – was similarly fixed.

Then came the realisation that our brains are *constantly* changing, and even more shockingly, that we have some control over the process.

London cab drivers are one of the most famous examples of how, through thought and practice, we can change the structure and function of our brains. Aspiring London taxi drivers must memorise an astounding number of navigational details about the city, including the names and locations of roughly 25,000 streets, 320 common routes through the city, and the "points of interest" that exist within a half a mile of each of these routes. Before being allowed to drive a taxi, would-be cabbies must pass a test that's so comprehensive that it's simply known as "The Knowledge". (And yes, they still have to do this, even now that we all have phones.)

In 2000, a team of researchers led by Eleanor Maguire at University College London published a study in which they scanned London cab drivers' brains to see how they compared to the brains of people who had *not* devoted months of their lives to memorising the intricacies of the city. The researchers discovered that the area responsible for spatial memories (the posterior hippocampus) was larger in the cab drivers' brains than in the non-cabbies'. The time they'd spent studying London's streets had had a physical impact. Their thoughts had changed their brains.

What's more, the longer a person had been a cab driver – in other words, the more time they'd spent *practicing* – the more noticeable the change.

Think about that for a second. And then think back to the fact that as of 2017, people in the UK were spending an estimated average of nearly two hours a day on their phones.

If you spend two hours a day doing *anything*, you're going to get pretty good at it. If I spent two hours a day practising the piano, I'd be able to accomplish my long-standing goal of learning to sight-read music within a couple of months. If I spent two hours a day studying Spanish, it wouldn't be long before I'd be able to have a basic conversation.

Our brains, just like those of the London cab drivers, respond powerfully to repetition and practice. So it's well worth investigating what skills the hours we're spending on our phones each day might be training us to develop – and at what cost.

MOST OF THE HOURS WE spend on our smartphones are not spent in concentrated thought. Instead, we're picking up our phones for minutes or seconds at a time.

Even when we're on them for longer stretches, we're not engrossed in one activity. We're scrolling and swiping between screens.

And even when we stay within one app – say, a news app or social media – we're usually still not focusing on anything for more than a few moments. Every tweet, message, profile, and post pulls our brains in a different direction. We end up acting like water bugs, skittering on the surface without ever diving in.

But that's not to say that we only casually focus our attention on our phones. On the contrary, they completely absorb us. The result is what seems like should be an oxymoron: an intensely focused state of distraction.

As it turns out, this type of frequent, focused distraction isn't just capable of creating long-lasting changes in our brains; it is *particularly* good at doing so.

In his 2010 book *The Shallows: What the Internet Is Doing to Our Brains*, journalist Nicholas Carr wrote that "[if] you were to set out to invent a medium that would rewire our mental circuits as quickly and thoroughly as possible, you would probably end up designing something that looks and works a lot like the internet".

Today, I'd argue that we can take this even further: if you wanted to invent a device that could rewire our minds, if you wanted to create a society of people who were perpetually distracted, isolated, and overtired, if you wanted to weaken our memories and damage our capacity for focus and deep thought, if you wanted to reduce empathy, encourage self-absorption, and redraw the lines of social etiquette, you'd likely end up with a smartphone.

YOUR PHONE IS
KILLING YOUR
ATTENTION SPAN

Multi-screening trains consumers to be less effective
at filtering out distractions – they are increasingly
hungry for something new. This means more
opportunities to hijack attention.

—Consumer Insights, Microsoft Canada, 2015

THE FIRST THING TO UNDERSTAND about our attention
spans is that distraction is our default. Human beings are
naturally distractible, because in nature, things are often
trying to kill us. We want our attention to be drawn to
changes in our environments, because those changes might
indicate a threat.

But why is staring at our phones so much more distracting and compelling than, say, scanning our surroundings for tigers? In *The Distracted Mind*, neuroscientist Adam Gazzaley and psychologist Larry Rosen suggest that it's because our phones (and, for that matter, the internet) satisfy another evolutionary quirk: our desire for information.

"Human beings seem to exhibit an innate drive to forage for information in much the same way that other animals are driven to forage for food," write Gazzaley and Rosen. "This 'hunger' is now fed to an extreme degree by modern technological advances that deliver highly accessible information."

In other words, our brains both prefer and are programmed to seek out and be distracted by new information. And that's exactly what our phones encourage them to do.

ONE OF THE REASONS OUR brains prefer distraction to concentration is that concentration requires our brains to do two difficult things at once.

The first is to choose what to pay attention to. That job falls to a part of the brain called the prefrontal cortex, which is responsible for so-called executive (or "top-down") functions, such as decision making and self-control.

In many ways, the prefrontal cortex is what makes us human. If we didn't have control over our attention, we couldn't think abstract and complicated thoughts.

But just like a muscle, the prefrontal cortex can become tired if we ask it to make too many decisions – a condition known as "decision fatigue". When our prefrontal cortex becomes tired, our focus wavers and our minds wander. We lose our ability to distinguish between what's important to pay attention to and what's not. The more information we're presented with, the more of a problem this becomes. (As a relatively new part of our brain, the prefrontal cortex is also one of the weakest. Under stressful conditions, it tends to freak out and hand the reins to more primitive areas of our brains – which is not a good thing, considering that we often reach for our phones out of stress.)

The second task required for concentration doesn't get as much, well, attention. But it's just as important – if not more so: we need to be able to ignore distractions.

Our brains are exposed to an onslaught of stimulation even *without* man-made distractions like phones (or interior distractions like thoughts). Sights, tastes, smells, sounds, textures – our senses are constantly presenting us with new information to act on and absorb.

In a way, this makes our ability to ignore distractions even more impressive than our ability to pay attention. We can pay attention to really only one thing at a time, but there is an infinite amount of sensory information that doing so might require us to block.

Unsurprisingly, ignoring distractions is tiring work, and the less we practice it, the worse at it we become. When our strength is exhausted and we can no longer block extraneous information, we lose our focus. We go back to our default state of distraction.

IF YOU'VE NOTICED THAT READING a book or printed newspaper doesn't feel the same as reading the same material on your phone or computer, you're not crazy. It's *not* the same.

When we read a book or the paper, most of the distractions we encounter are external – a barking dog, or the sound of a vacuum cleaner. This makes it relatively easy for our brains to decide what's important and to ignore what's not.

This also leaves our brains with plenty of available bandwidth to think about and absorb what we're reading. When we read words in print – which is to say, without links or ads – we primarily activate the brain areas associated with absorbing and understanding information.

But when we read on a phone or computer, links and ads are everywhere. (For now at least, most ebooks are a glorious exception.) From the point of view of our attention spans, this is problematic in at least three ways.

First, every time we encounter a link, our brains must make a split-second decision about whether to click on it. These decisions are so frequent and tiny that we often don't even notice that they're happening. But we can't make split-second decisions and think deeply at the same time – the two acts use different and competing brain regions. Every decision, no matter how tiny or subconscious, pulls our attention away from what we are reading. This in turn makes it harder to absorb the content of what we're reading – let alone to think about it critically, or remember it later.

Second, unlike a dog barking in the background, online distractions are embedded in what we're trying to focus on. This makes it very difficult for our brains to distinguish between what to pay attention to and what to ignore. Trying to absorb the meaning of a word without noticing its link is like trying to count a dog's whiskers while the dog is licking your face: nearly impossible, and almost definitely unpleasant.

And third, when mental fatigue causes us to give in to our brains' natural preference for distraction – whether it's by falling for clickbait or swiping over to social media – we reinforce the same mental circuits that made it hard to sustain our focus to begin with. We get better at *not* staying focused.

The result is that, the more we read online, the more we teach our brains to skim. This can be a useful skill to hone, especially when we're constantly faced with such information overload. But it becomes a problem if skimming becomes our default – because the better we become at skimming, the worse we get at reading and thinking more deeply. And the harder it is for us to focus on just one thing.

UNFORTUNATELY, THE WORSE OUR FOCUS gets, the more valuable we become. Just as social media companies make money by stealing (and then selling) your attention, informational websites make money by distracting you. Even subscription-based sites, such as newspapers, depend on page views and click-throughs for revenue. That's why online articles contain so many links and why slideshows are so common. Focus isn't profitable. Distraction is.

8

YOUR PHONE
MESSES WITH
YOUR MEMORY

*What you have discovered is a recipe
not for memory, but for reminder.*

—Plato, *Phaedrus*

OUR BRAINS HAVE TWO PRIMARY forms of memory –
short-term and long-term – and our phones affect both.

Long-term memory is often described as being like a
filing cabinet. According to this analogy, when you want to
remember something, your brain does a quick search of its
archives and retrieves that one specific memory from the
folder in which it was stored, leaving the rest of the files
untouched.

But that's not how it works. When we store a long-term memory, it doesn't exist on its own in a manila folder in our brain. It exists in a network of other connected memories. Called "schemas", these networks help us make sense of the world by linking every piece of new information that we acquire to information that we already have. Schemas explain why a single stimulus – say, the smell of a cake baking – can trigger a flurry of memories.

Schemas also sharpen our thinking by helping us identify commonalities between seemingly disparate things. For example, our brains know that a traffic cone and a pumpkin have different purposes – and thus the two objects aren't connected schematically by function. But traffic cones and pumpkins do share a different trait: they're both orange. This means that they're schematically linked by colour, both to each other and to other orange things, such as tangerines.

As this example demonstrates, every piece of information can exist in multiple schemas at once. Tangerines are linked to the schema for the colour orange (and thus share a connection with a traffic cone) *and* the schema for citrus fruit (thus sharing a connection with a lemon).

The number of connections is itself important, because the more you're able to draw connections between seemingly unconnected things, the more likely you are to have insights. One thought triggers another thought, which triggers another . . . and suddenly, you've had a breakthrough.

In short: the more nuanced and detailed your schemas are, the greater your capacity for complex thought. But schemas take time – and mental space – to build. When our brains are overloaded, our ability to create schemas suffers. And guess what overloads our brain?

TO UNDERSTAND WHY HEAVY PHONE use messes with our schemas, we need to talk about working memory (a term that's often used interchangeably with *short-term memory*).

Broadly speaking, your working memory is everything you're holding in your mind at any given moment. It's the part of your mind that answers the question, "What was I just looking for?" when you walk into a room in search of your keys and get distracted along the way.

Working memory – which can also be thought of as your consciousness – is also the gateway through which every long-term memory must pass. After all, you can't have a long-term memory of an experience unless you were conscious of it in the first place.

Here's the first problem: our working memory can't hold on to many things at once. A famous 1956 study on working memory was titled "The Magical Number Seven, Plus or Minus Two" (suggesting that we're able to hold between five and nine items in our working memory) – but more recent estimates put the capacity closer to two to four.

As a result of their limited capacities, our working memories are easily overloaded. If I introduce you to two people at a party, you probably will be able to remember their names. But if I introduce you to eight people at once, you probably won't. Likewise, it'd be harder to remember your own phone number if it were presented as an uninterrupted string of digits instead of in three distinct chunks.

Adding to the challenge, the more information your working memory is trying to handle – which is referred to as your "cognitive load" – the less likely you are to remember any of it.

That's in part because it takes time and mental energy to transfer information from your working memory to your long-term memory. (In fact, whereas short-term memories are generally created by strengthening the connection between neural circuits, creating long-term memories requires your brain to actually create new proteins.) It also takes time and mental energy to connect each new piece of information to all the schemas of which it could be a part. If your brain is busy trying to hold too much information in its working memory – if its cognitive load is too great – it won't have the ability to store that information, let alone process it in a way that makes it useful, or to create the proteins necessary to transfer the memory into long-term storage. It's like trying to organise your wallet while juggling: you can't.

And that brings us to our phones: everything about smartphones overloads our working memories. The apps, the emails, the news feeds, the headlines, even the home screen itself – a smartphone is a virtual avalanche of information.

The result, short term, is mental fatigue and difficulty concentrating. The long-term consequences are even scarier. As we've talked about, when we train our attention on our phones, we miss out on everything else going on around us – and if you don't have an experience to begin with, then it goes without saying that you're not going to remember it later.

What's more, when we overload our working memories, we make it harder for our brains to transfer new information to our long-term memories. This in turn makes it less likely that we'll remember the experiences (and information) that we *did* manage to pay attention to.

Lastly, when our working memories are overloaded and our cognitive loads are too great, our brains don't have the resources necessary to connect new information and experiences to our pre-existing schemas. Not only does this reduce the likelihood of those memories becoming permanent, but the weaker our schemas become, the less likely we are to have insights and ideas. We lose our capacity for deep thought.

9

STRESS, SLEEP AND

SATISFACTION

*In their quest for happiness, people mistake
excitement of the mind for real happiness.*

—Sayadaw U Pandita, *In This Very Life: The Liberation
Teachings of the Buddha*

IN THE PAST, if a person described herself as feeling happy, sad, excited, anxious, curious, frustrated, ignored, important, lonely, joyful, and existentially depressed within the space of five minutes, she likely would have received a diagnosis.

But give me five minutes on my phone, and I can accomplish this and more. Our phones are like Pandora's boxes of emotions – and every time we check them, we open ourselves up to an unpleasant surprise. You could get an email that worries you or a text message about something you forgot to do. Maybe there's a news story that makes you angry.

Or a stock price that makes you anxious. Or a post that makes you sad.

A lot of the time, you'll end up feeling stressed about something you truly cannot control, like politics or stock prices. But in a way, situations in which you *could* take back control – say, by answering that stressful email right then and there – are even worse: in order to restore your sense of equilibrium, you have to remove yourself from whatever experience you had been having.

In short, if ignorance is bliss, 'tis folly to look at your phone.

YOUR PHONE AND YOUR SLEEP

Every night, two to three hours before your bedtime, a tiny gland in your brain begins to release a hormone called melatonin. Melatonin tells your body that it's nighttime and makes you sleepy.

When daylight, which is a blue light, hits the back of your eyes in the morning, your brain stops producing melatonin. You feel awake and ready to start your day. When blue light fades (and is replaced by darkness or the yellow glow of incandescent bulbs), melatonin begins to be released again.

Guess what else radiates blue light? Screens. When we use our phones or tablets or computers before bed, their blue light tells our brains that it is daytime and that we should be awake. In other words, when we check our phones at night, we're giving ourselves jet lag. Screen time, particularly in the hour before bedtime, both keeps us up later and harms the quality of our sleep.

But the quality of light is just one way that our phones affect our sleep cycles. Most of the things we do on our phones – reading the news, playing games – are stimulating activities. Imagine how difficult it would be to doze off if all of the people you follow on social media were in the room with you, the television was blaring in the background, and several friends were having a political debate. That's essentially what you're doing when you bring your phone into bed with you.

Phones' effects on sleep are particularly concerning when you consider the health consequences of chronic fatigue, which include increased risk of obesity, diabetes, cardiovascular disease, and even early death.

Indeed, according to the Division of Sleep Medicine at Harvard Medical School, even short-term sleep deprivation "can affect judgment, mood, ability to learn and retain information, and may increase the risk of serious accidents and injury". When you're tired, it's harder for your brain to filter out distractions. You have poorer self-control. You're less able to tolerate frustration. And your brain has difficulty deciding what's important to pay attention to and what's not.

And short-term sleep deprivation doesn't require you to have one crazy night. Even just a week and a half's worth of sleeping six hours a night (instead of seven to nine) can, according to the Division of Sleep Medicine, "result in the same level of impairment on the tenth day as being awake for the previous 24 hours straight" – which is to say that it can induce "impairments in performance equivalent to those induced by a blood-alcohol level of 0.10 percent".

Oh, and if you're thinking that this obviously does not apply to you, keep in mind that the more sleep-deprived people are, the more vigorously they may insist that they are not – possibly because their ability to judge their own mental state has been impaired.

YOUR PHONE AND FLOW

Flow is a term coined by the psychologist Mihaly Csikszentmihalyi to describe the feeling you get when you're completely and totally engaged in an experience. People can experience flow when they're singing, playing sports or even working. When you're in flow, you're so present in the moment that you feel as if you're outside of time. The line between your experience and your mind gets erased. You're un-self-conscious. You're entirely absorbed. You're in the zone. Flow leads to the sorts of moments and memories that make life seem rich.

If you're distracted, you can't immerse yourself in an experience – which means that you can't, by definition, get into flow. And since our phones are tools of distraction, this means that the more we spend on our phones, the less likely we are to experience it.

YOUR PHONE AND CREATIVITY

Creativity – that is, the process of coming up with new ideas – also requires relaxation and mental space, both of which are hard to come by when we're on our phones. Creativity requires you to be well rested – as Judith Owens, director of Sleep Medicine at Children's National Medical Center in

Washington, D.C., has said, "Sleep deprivation can affect memory, creativity, verbal creativity, and even things like judgment and motivation." And creativity is often sparked by boredom, which is another mental state that our phones are great at helping us avoid.

To me, the importance of boredom to creativity is summed up by this quote from Lin-Manuel Miranda, the award-winning, crazy-talented genius behind *Hamilton: An American Musical*: "I remember when I was a kid, I was in a three-hour car ride with my best friend, Danny," Miranda told an interviewer for *GQ*. "Before we got in the car, he grabbed a stick from his front yard, and the entire drive home he made up games with this . . . *stick*. Sometimes the stick was a man, sometimes a piece in a larger game, or he'd give it voices, pretend the stick was a telephone. I remember sitting there next to him with my Donkey Kong thinking, *Dude, you just entertained yourself for three hours . . . with a f-ing* twig! And I thought to myself, *Wow, I have to raise my imagination game*."

When I read this, part of me thinks that I should be spending more time playing with sticks. And another, more cynical part of me thinks, "I bet someone is going to make an app for that."

10

HOW TO TAKE
BACK YOUR LIFE

We learn to stay with the uneasiness, the
tightening, the itch of [our cravings]. We train
in sitting still with our desire to scratch. This is
how we learn to stop the chain reaction of habitual
patterns that otherwise will rule our lives.

—Pema Chödrön

SO HERE'S THE GOOD NEWS: we can undo many of our
phones' negative effects. We can rebuild our attention spans.
We can get our focus back. We can reduce our stress, improve
our memories, and reclaim a good night's sleep. We can
change our relationships with our phones and take back our
lives from our devices. That's what the next part of the book –
"The Breakup" – is designed to help you do. Before we move
on, though, let's talk a bit about the science and philosophy
behind the break-up's steps.

MINDFULNESS

Mindfulness is a complicated word to define, but for our purposes, I like the definition put forth by Judson Brewer, director of research at the Center for Mindfulness in Medicine, Health Care, and Society at the University of Massachusetts Medical School: "Mindfulness is about seeing the world more clearly" – including ourselves.

This simple idea is actually quite powerful – especially when it comes to breaking addictions. How powerful? In 2011, Brewer and his colleagues published the results of a randomised, controlled trial designed to test whether mindfulness training could help people stop smoking. More specifically, they wanted to compare mindfulness to the accepted "gold standard" treatment: the American Lung Association's "Freedom from Smoking" programme.

Over the course of two years, Brewer randomised nearly a hundred smokers into two groups. One group was assigned to participate in the Freedom from Smoking treatment. The other group was trained in mindfulness.

First, Brewer taught the "mindful" smokers about habit loops. They learned to identify their triggers and practised paying attention to their cravings (and reactions) without trying to change anything. This step alone was surprisingly effective – just paying conscious attention to the *taste* of cigarettes, for example, was enough to give one longtime smoker the resolve to finally quit. "She moved from wisdom to knowledge," writes Brewer, "from knowing in her head that smoking was bad to *knowing* it in her bones."

Next, he taught them to turn toward their cravings, rather than to run away. Participants practised recognising their cravings and relaxing into them – that is, allowing them to happen without trying to stop them. They practiced paying attention to how their cravings made them emotionally and physically feel, and they used this practice as a way to "ride out" their cravings when they occurred. Brewer also taught participants formal meditation exercises that they were expected to do each day.

When Brewer's data were analysed, it turned out that the people who had received the mindfulness training had quit at *twice the rate* of the Freedom from Smoking group. What's more, far fewer people from the mindfulness group relapsed.

Practicing mindfulness can be just as effective – if not more so – when it comes to breaking our addictions to our phones. But that's not all it can do. Paying deliberate attention to your moment-to-moment experience also gives you more fodder for memories that don't involve your phone. It helps you deal with anxiety. It adds richness to your life. And that's why practising this form of mindfulness is one of the first things that we're going to learn how to do.

We'll start by paying deliberate attention to our emotions, thoughts and reactions without judging ourselves or trying to change anything. We'll notice the invitations that our minds are sending us. And then we'll practise deciding how – and if – we want to respond.

Let me take a second to elaborate: like overzealous (and slightly deranged) party planners, our minds are *constantly* presenting us with invitations to do certain things or to react in certain ways. You hit a traffic jam and your mind invites you to give a fellow motorist the finger. You find yourself alone on a Friday night and your mind invites you to conclude that you are worthless and you have no friends.

In other words, what we think of as irresistible impulses are actually invitations being sent by our minds. This is an important insight because once you recognise this, you can ask your mind why it's inviting you to such crappy parties. Why couldn't a traffic jam be an invitation to a mobile karaoke session? Why couldn't a solitary Friday night be an invitation to watch a film that you can't convince anyone else to see?

Not only does mindfulness help us get better at noticing and managing our invitations, but it also enables us to recognise the core emotions, fears and desires that are driving our addictions – which is an essential step in breaking them. As Brewer explains in *The Craving Mind*, most addictions stem from a desire to feel better and/or to make a bad feeling go away. If you try to cut back on your phone use without first figuring out what you're trying to achieve or avoid, you're dooming yourself to failure. Either you're going to relapse, or you're going to find another, potentially more destructive habit that achieves the same effect.

The more you practise being mindful, the more it becomes obvious that your brain has a mind of its own. (I like to think of my mind as a good friend who also happens to be totally crazy.) The moment you recognise that you don't have to say yes to every invitation is the moment you gain control over your life – both on and off your phone.

HOW TO RIDE OUT
YOUR PHONE CRAVINGS

The same approach that worked so well for the smokers also works for our phones. If we simply acknowledge our discomfort without trying to fight against it – in other words, if we ride out the wave – our cravings will eventually fade on their own.

For example, let's say you catch yourself reaching for your phone. Practising mindfulness means that instead of trying to fight your urge or criticising yourself for having it, you simply notice the urge and stay present with it as it unfolds. As it does, you can ask questions about it. What does the craving feel like in your brain and in your body? Why are you having this particular urge right now? What reward are you hoping to receive, or what discomfort are you trying to avoid? What would happen if you reacted to the impulse? What would happen if you did nothing at all?

The next time you find yourself tempted to look at your phone, pause instead. Take a breath and just *notice* the craving. Don't give in to it, but don't try to make it go away. Observe it. See what happens.

"[W]e must act, individually and collectively, to make our attention our own again, and so reclaim ownership of the very experience of living."

—Tim Wu, *The Attention Merchants*

part ii

THE

BREAK-

UP

TECHNOLOGY

TRIAGE

Everyone knows what attention is. It is the taking
possession by the mind, in clear and vivid form, of
one out of what seem several simultaneously possible
objects of trains of thought . . . It implies withdrawal
from some things in order to deal effectively with
others, and is a condition which has a real opposite in
the confused, dazed, scatterbrained state.

—William James, *The Principles of Psychology*

WELCOME TO THE BREAK-UP, your hands-on guide to
creating a new relationship with your phone. Here are some
notes before we begin.

You can personalise the plan. I have structured the break-up
as the 30-day guided plan outlined in the box – and I do recommend spreading it out, because it takes time to change
habits. That said, you should feel free to use this guide any

way you want. The whole point is for the experience – and your new relationship – to be personalised.

WEEK 1: TECHNOLOGY TRIAGE

Day 1 (Monday): Download a Tracking App

Day 2 (Tuesday): Assess Your Current Relationship

Day 3 (Wednesday): Start Paying Attention

Day 4 (Thursday): Take Stock and Take Action

Day 5 (Friday): Delete Social Media Apps

Day 6 (Saturday): Come Back to (Real) Life

Day 7 (Sunday): Get Physical

WEEK 2: CHANGING YOUR HABITS

Day 8 (Monday): Say "No" to Notifications

Day 9 (Tuesday): The Life-Changing Magic of Tidying Apps

Day 10 (Wednesday): Change Where You Charge It

Day 11 (Thursday): Set Yourself Up for Success

Day 12 (Friday): Download an App-Blocker

Day 13 (Saturday): Set Boundaries (No-Phone Zones and Wake-Up Times)

Day 14 (Sunday): Stop Phubbing

WEEK 3: RECLAIMING YOUR BRAIN

Day 15 (Monday): Stop, Breathe, and Be

Day 16 (Tuesday): Practise Pausing

You are not alone. The italicised quotes are from other people who have already gone through the breakup. I'm including them both as a source of inspiration and as proof that we're all struggling with similar things.

There is no judgment in this breakup. Not by you, and certainly not by me. Our job is simply to observe, to ask questions, and to experiment. If you conclude that sending 150 WhatsApp messages a day is how you want to be spending your time, that is entirely your call.

There is no need to stress – and there's no way to "fail". If you try an exercise and it works for you, great: add it to your toolkit. If an exercise doesn't work for you, then just move on to the next one. Likewise, if you slip back into an old habit – which, let's be honest, is likely to happen – don't beat yourself up. Instead, just get back on track. One way to do this is to simply acknowledge that you're disappointed, and then do something to offset the behavior you feel bad about and to regain momentum – kind of like a carbon offset, but with your phone. For example, if you fell into a social media black hole when you woke up, you could make a deliberate point of making lunch plans with a real-life friend, or going for an evening walk without your phone.

Take notes. The break-up includes prompts and questions for you to answer. If you're the journaling type, I encourage you to create a special phone break-up notebook, so that by the end of this experiment you'll have a written record of your thoughts to look back on. You could also write your answers as a series of emails or letters to yourself, or jot notes in the margins.

Seek further instructions. Given how quickly technology changes, I am deliberately not going into nitty-gritty detail about how to change specific settings. If you're confused, do an internet search and include your smartphone model. Or just find the nearest nine-year-old and have her do it for you.

Start with the personal. We're going to focus on the ways we use our phones in our personal lives (as opposed to for work or school purposes). This is for two reasons. First, it's low-hanging fruit. Many people excuse their phone habits by claiming that they need to check their phones all the time for work. But are you *really* checking for work? Or are you "checking for work" by looking at your Instagram feed? Second, any change we make to the personal use of our phones is likely to affect our work use as well. If you fix your personal relationship with your phone, you may find that a better professional relationship with it falls into place, too.

INVITE OTHER PEOPLE

You're going to have more fun – and your new relationship is more likely to stick – if you do the breakup with another person (or people). I encourage you to recruit a friend or family member or roommate or colleague or book club, and go through the breakup together. That way you can use the book's questions as conversational prompts, and keep each other on track.

"Whenever possible, people should encourage other people to join them – and make an event out of it. Like dieting, it's easier when you make the change to healthy eating with your partner or family." —SARAH

There is nothing wrong with mindless distraction. There are times when zoning out on your phone is exactly what you want to do. What *is* problematic – and what we're trying to avoid – is letting a state of mindless distraction become our default.

And last, but not least:

The point is not to punish yourself. We're trying to resolve discrepancies between how we *say* we want to live our lives, and how we are actually living our lives. Sure, there may be some uncomfortable moments along the way, but ultimately, breaking up with your phone should make you feel good. If you start feeling like all you're doing is saying "no" to yourself, then take a step back to regroup. Our goal isn't abstinence; it's consciousness.

WHY A TECHNOLOGY TRIAGE?

When phone break-ups fail, it's usually due to a lack of preparation. As we've touched on, people tend to try to change their relationships with their phones without first asking themselves what they actually *want* their relationships with their phones to be. They start with a vague goal – "I want to spend less time on my phone" – without specifying what they're actually trying to change or accomplish, or identifying why they reach for their phones to begin with. Then they try to go cold turkey, and end up feeling discouraged and powerless when it doesn't work.

This is the equivalent of dumping someone because you say you want a "better relationship" – but, when pressed, admitting that you actually have no idea what that better relationship would look like. If you don't take the time to figure that out, you are highly likely to end up in a relationship that's just as unsatisfying or unhealthy as the one that you just got out of.

The all-or-nothing approach to smartphones also totally ignores the fact that, as we've discussed before, there are many *good* things about our phones. The point of breaking up with our phones isn't to deprive ourselves of the benefits of modern technology. It's to set boundaries so that we can enjoy the good parts of our phones while also protecting ourselves from the bad.

That's why we need to do a Technology Triage. In this stage, we'll use mindfulness – and apps – to gather data about our current relationships with our phones so that we can identify what's working, what's not, and what we want to change.

OUR GUIDING QUESTION

We've talked about how, both literally and metaphorically, **our lives are what we pay attention to.** So please take a moment right now to answer this question:

What do you want to pay attention to?

I encourage you to continue to come back to this question throughout the course of our 30 days together (and beyond). Use it to ground yourself any time you feel yourself reaching for your phone – or any other moment when you feel as if you've lost your way.

"I want to pay attention to my surroundings. I want to notice nature, and art, and my own feelings." —EMILY

"I want to pay attention to friends: when we're experiencing something together (like a movie or a meal), I want to be fully present." —LAUREN

USE YOUR LOCK SCREEN AS A REMINDER

You may want to write "What do you want to pay attention to?" on a piece of paper, take a photo of it, and set it as the lock screen for your phone. (You could even take a photo of someone you love holding the piece of paper.) That way, whenever you reach for your phone, you'll be reminded to check in with yourself first.

SCHEDULE IT

Before we officially begin, I'd also like to take advantage of what is hopefully a high level of motivation to get you to pick a date for your Trial Separation. Right now. I'm serious: fetch your calendar and schedule it.

If you follow my suggested plan and start your break-up on a Monday, you'll be doing the Trial Separation sometime during the third weekend of the break-up. I recommend Friday evening to Saturday evening because it sets a nice tone for the rest of the weekend, but Saturday to Sunday is fine, too (and if that weekend doesn't work for you, you can pick another twenty-four-hour period).

Yes, you can change this date later if you want or need to. The point is to increase the chances that you'll actually do it, rather than just read about it, by putting a date in your calendar way ahead of time. It'll also give you time to prepare. (I'll give you lots of help preparing for the Trial Separation. We will hold each other, and it will be okay. In fact, you may be surprised by how much you enjoy it.)

Also, consider adding the entire break-up to your calendar, either on or off your phone. If you don't feel like adding 30 individual events to your calendar, set a single reminder – something along the lines of "Break Up with My Phone" – to repeat each day for 30 days.

DAY 1 (MONDAY)
DOWNLOAD A TRACKING APP

The first step in our Technology Triage is to compare the amount of time we *think* we're spending on our phones to how much time we're actually spending on our phones. Start by jotting down your answers to these questions:

- If you had to guess, how many times a day do you think you pick up your phone?

- How much time do you estimate that you spend on it per day?

Next, download a time-tracking app that will automatically monitor how often you reach for your phone and how long you spend on it (see Recommended Resources, page 169, for specific suggestions).

Don't try to change anything yet about your behaviour; our goal is just to gather data. We'll touch base about your results in a few days.

"Realising the disparity between how much time I thought I spent on the phone each day and how much time I actually spent on it was huge." —DUSTIN

DAY 2 (TUESDAY)
ASSESS YOUR CURRENT RELATIONSHIP

Now that you've got a tracking app up and running in the background, pull out a notebook or create a new email message to yourself (or just get a pen and write in the margins – I won't be offended) and write a few sentences in response to the following questions:

- What do you love about your phone?
- What don't you love about your phone?
- What changes do you notice in yourself – positive or negative – when you spend a lot of time on your phone? (Depending on how old you are, you can also ask yourself if you've noticed any changes since you got a smartphone to begin with.)

"I love having the world's information at my fingertips. The ability to answer any question or find my way to any place is pretty remarkable. [But] it is too easy to pull it out and start reading news and checking things, when previously I would have just observed the world around me. The times I force myself to do that I always notice something interesting that I'd otherwise miss." —CONOR

"My attention span has significantly lessened. I don't make an effort to plan ahead (either for directions or info) because I know I can always look it up at the last minute. My memory is weaker. I have noticed physical discomfort from looking down on my phone and texting a lot (neck, thumbs, wrists)." —ERIN

Next, imagine yourself a month from now, at the end of your break-up. What would you like your new relationship with your phone to look like? What would you like to have done or accomplished with your extra time? What would you like someone to say if you asked them to describe how you'd changed? Write your future self a brief note or email describing what success would look like, and/or congratulating yourself for achieving it.

"I would like myself to not be so tied to my phone. To not spend hours scrolling through pages of people I don't really know. I would like to have used the time I've gained back for something useful. Started a new hobby, gone to an extra gym class. I'd like my boyfriend/friends to say that I am much more engaged in everything. Less distracted." —SIOBHAN

DAY 3 (WEDNESDAY)
START PAYING ATTENTION

The next step of the Technology Triage is to continue your mindfulness practice by paying attention to how and when you use your phone, and how you feel when you do so.

Over the next twenty-four hours, try to notice:

- Situations in which you nearly always find yourself using your phone. (For example, waiting in a queue, in the lift, in the car.) Also note the first time in the morning and the last time in the evening that you typically look at your phone.

- How your posture changes when using your phone.

- Your emotional state right *before* you reach for your phone. (For example: bored, curious, anxious, happy, lonely, excited, sad, loving, and so on.)

- Your emotional state right *after* you use your phone (Do you feel better? Worse? Did your phone satisfy whatever emotional need caused you to reach for it?)

- How, and how often, your phone grabs your attention (via notifications, texts, and the like).

- How you feel while you are using your phone – as well as how you feel when you realise that you *don't* have your phone. The point here is to start to become aware of when and how your phone triggers your brain to release dopamine and cortisol – and what you feel like when that happens. (Very generally speaking, cravings are a desire for dopamine, dopamine itself feels exciting, and cortisol feels like anxiety.)

I'd also like you to pay attention to:

- Moments – either on or off your phone – when you feel some combination of engaged, energised, joyful, effective, and purposeful. When that happens, notice what you were doing, whom you were with, and whether your phone was involved.

- How and when *other* people use their phones – and how it makes you feel.

Lastly, I'd like you to choose several moments in your day when you are mostly likely to pick up your phone, and see if you can identify a consistent trigger that makes you repeat this habit. For example, maybe you check your phone first thing in the morning because you're anxious. Or maybe it's just because it's on your bedside table. Maybe you check your phone in the lift because everyone else is also checking their phone. Maybe you check it at work because you're bored with whatever you're supposed to be doing.

We're not trying to make a judgment on any of these triggers; we're just trying to become aware of them so that we can begin to identify patterns.

As a warm-up, try this slightly modified version of a "phone meditation" exercise suggested by David Levy, author of *Mindful Tech: How to Bring Balance to Our Digital Lives.*

First, notice how you feel right now. How is your breathing? Your posture? Your sense of focus? Your general emotional state?

Now take out your phone and hold it in your hand without unlocking the screen. Notice any changes in your breathing, posture, focus and emotional state.

Next, actually unlock the screen and open one of the apps you use the most frequently (for example, email, social media or the news). Spend a few moments scrolling through the feed. If you're looking at email, answer a message. Then scan yourself again for any changes.

Lastly, turn off the phone and put it away, out of sight. How do you feel? Is anything different?

Personally, I've noticed that while it can initially be pleasant, I hardly ever feel better after I use my phone – an observation that has helped me catch myself when I'm about to pick it up out of habit.

> "I notice that I'm usually feeling a little anxious before I pick it up. It's not that five minutes earlier I was anxious; it's that for whatever reason, I'm picking up the phone and feel anxious in that moment of picking it up to check it. Then I usually relax once I've logged in and checked email and Facebook. Why?" – JENNY

CREATE A PHYSICAL PROMPT

To help you notice when you reach for your phone, put a rubber band or hair tie around your phone or a piece of tape or a sticker on the back. That way, any time you reach for your phone, you'll feel the prompt and be reminded to pay attention. You'll probably need the reminder for only a few days; after a while, the noticing will become more automatic. You can also do something visual, such as changing the image on your lock screen to a picture of a piece of paper that says "Notice!" or "Why did you pick me up?"

TAKE STOCK AND TAKE ACTION

By now, we've tracked our phone usage for a few days. Now that we've gathered this data, let's analyse it.

1. LOOK AT THE RESULTS FROM THE TRACKING APP YOU INSTALLED

The tracking data may not be entirely accurate, but that's okay – we're just trying to get a general sense of how our guesses match up to reality.

How many times per day did you pick up your phone, and how much time did you spend on it? How does this compare to your guesses? What, if anything, surprised you?

> *"I've been horrified by the data that [the tracking app] has been providing. Yesterday I picked up my phone eighty-one times and spent over two hours on it."* —SAMANTHA

2. NOTICE WHAT YOU'VE NOTICED

Next, think about what you've noticed over the past twenty-four hours about when and why you typically use your phone. What did you notice about how – and how often – your phone interrupts you, or does something that grabs your attention? How did these interruptions make you feel?

> *"[Interruptions] happen all the time. All. The. Time. They generally feel sort of like a coffee buzz – energising, edgy, and ephemeral."* —JOSH

What did you notice about how your felt physically and emotionally before, during, and after you used your phone, and during times when you were separated from it? For example, did you feel relaxed, tense, excited, anxious, or some other emotion? What did you pick up on about how your phone affects your levels of dopamine and cortisol?

> *"Before reaching for the phone, I feel a slight twinge of discomfort, of wanting something – like I might feel if I were sitting at the kitchen table and suddenly thought of food, even though I wasn't hungry. I also feel a slightly giddy sense of anticipation, like I used to when I went to the post office with my mum, hoping a pen pal had written."*
> —JESSICA

What did you notice about the moments when you felt you were in a state of "flow" (that is, some combination of engaged, energised, joyful, effective and purposeful)? What were you doing? Whom you were with? Was your phone involved?

> *"It sounds so simple, but I felt all those things when I was weeding the garden. I love being outdoors, and I felt effective and purposeful as I watched the pile of weeds grow larger. My phone was only involved when I took a picture to send to some friends who are equally nerdy about plants."* —JENNY

How did you feel when you saw other people on their phones?

> *"I really hate the shifting of etiquette that has made it okay for people to use their phones during the workday – under the guise that they're having frantic work-related exchanges when obviously it's all personal."* —BETH

Putting this all together, what patterns did you notice? What, if anything, surprised you?

> *"I use the phone mostly when I'm bored (going from one place to another, or sitting down on my own) or at night when sitting on the couch (while watching TV or procrastinating). I don't think much about it in the moment, but in hindsight I realise it's a lot of time I could be using on more productive things." —BERNARDO*

3. CREATE YOUR FIRST SPEED BUMP

One of the most effective ways to regain control over our phones is to build speed bumps: small obstacles that force us to slow down. By creating a pause between our impulses and our actions, speed bumps give us the chance to change course if we decide we want to take a different route.

We'll be experimenting with a lot of mental and physical speed bumps over the course of our break-up. The first is an exercise that I call WWW, which is short for *What For, Why Now, and What Else.* (You might want to consider putting "WWW" on your lock screen as a reminder.)

DAY 5 (FRIDAY)
DELETE SOCIAL MEDIA APPS

As we've discussed, social media is like junk food: bingeing on it makes us feel bad, and yet once we start consuming it, it's really hard to stop. So let's take control of it.

WWW: WHAT FOR, WHY NOW, AND WHAT ELSE

Any time you notice that you are about to reach for your phone, take a second to ask yourself:

What For? What are you picking up your phone to do? (For example, to check your email, browse Amazon, order dinner, kill time, and so on.)

Why Now? Why are you picking up your phone now instead of later? The reason might be practical (I want to take a photo), situational (I'm in the lift), or emotional (I want a distraction).

What Else? What else could you do right now besides check your phone?

If you do your Ws, and then decide that you really *do* want to use your phone right now, that's totally fine. The point is simply to give yourself a chance to explore your options for that particular moment, so that if and when you turn your attention to your phone, it's the result of a conscious decision.

Identifying your goal ahead of time also prevents an impulse to share a photo on social media from devolving into another thirty minutes spent absent-mindedly scrolling through your feed.

First, take a moment to think about which social media platforms you use the most. Then ask yourself how much money *per week* you would be willing to pay for each of them.

Seriously, think about this for a second.

Then, when you've got a number in mind, think back on a recent experience that was really rewarding or fun – such as spending time with a group of your best friends or doing something that you love.

If we could go back in time, how much would I have to pay you to get you to knowingly miss out on that experience?

Got it?

If you're like most people, the amount you'd pay for social media is quite low – most people's answers hover somewhere around a dollar a week per platform.

In contrast, most people's rates for knowingly missing out on fun were much, *much* higher.

One obvious conclusion is that we value social media much less than we do real-life fun – and that we should probably prioritize the latter. Fair enough. But for some people, social media is an enjoyable tool that makes them feel connected to friends, family, and the world around us.

Ideally, we'd be able to use social media in moderation, enjoying the good parts without risking the bad. But this is particularly difficult to do on our phones because, as we've discovered, social media *apps* are specifically designed to suck us in.

Thankfully, there's an easy way to fight back: **delete all social media apps from your phone.**

I'm serious. Do it now. Put your finger on an app icon until it starts jiggling, and then press the x in the corner.

The app, panicking, will respond with a manipulative question ("Are you really sure you want to delete me and all my data?"). Say yes and then shake your head in disgust: everyone knows that Facebook didn't *really* delete any of your data. It's all still lurking in the cloud, ready to be used against you and reinstalled/downloaded at any time.

If you are hesitating, let's be clear about two things:

1. This is not an irreversible decision. Ideally, I would like you to keep these apps off your phone until we reach the "make-up" part of our experiment (at which point I will provide suggestions for how to create a healthier relationship with social media). But I'm not the boss of you.

2. You can still check social media whenever you want. I'm not trying to get you off social media entirely; I just want you to check it through your phone or computer's internet browser instead of on an app.

The point, again, is to create speed bumps. Browser versions of social media platforms often have fewer features than their apps and are clunkier to use. So they provide lots of opportunities to ask yourself whether you really want to be checking social media at that moment.

If you decide that you do, that's fine – but check it in a structured way. Define your purpose ahead of time (Are you posting something? Looking for something specific? Just scrolling for fun?) and decide how long you want to spend. You may even want to set a timer. Then, when you're done, log out and close the window so that it won't open automatically the next time you launch the browser.

In short: just do it. Delete the apps for now. *You will be okay.* I promise. In fact, many people have told me that, in terms of breaking their addiction to their phones, this was one of the most useful things they did.

WHAT TO DO IF YOU'RE AFRAID YOU'LL FORGET YOUR PASSWORDS

I'm going to be suggesting that you experiment with deleting lots of apps during our time together. If you're like me, you may find yourself hesitating – not because you necessarily care about the app, but because you're worried that you won't be able to find/ remember your password if you decide to reinstall it. The solution is to finally do what all those internet security people have been telling us for years, and sign up for a password manager. Password managers are apps that store all your passwords (they can also generate new ones for you that are harder to break). You set one master password for the password manager, and then, when you want to sign into a site/ app, the manager will do it for you. This makes it less likely that your data will be hacked, and also will give you the freedom to play around with deleting things without worrying.

Also, here's an interesting psychological trick for you: researchers have found that the vocabulary you use to describe a new habit has a strong effect on the likelihood that you'll stick with it. To be specific, saying that you "do" or "don't" do something – framing an action as part of your identity – is much more effective than saying that you "have to" or "can't" do something. (For example, saying, "I go to the gym five days a week", compared to saying, "I *have* to go to the gym five days a week.")

This is a great opportunity to experiment with this trick. Right now, you are a person who does not have social media apps on your phone. So when you feel the urge to open or reinstall one of the apps, don't try to resist it by saying that you "can't" or aren't "allowed" to do so. Instead, simply describe your current reality: "I do not keep social media apps on my phone." This simple shift can make a surprising difference.

Oh, and lastly, make a point of taking some of the time you usually spend on social media and spending it with people you care about instead – *offline*. Call a friend. Invite someone to coffee. Have a party. (Yes, you can use social media to help you organise.) Notice how you feel afterwards, especially compared to how you usually feel after spending time on social media.

> "Instagram and Facebook are the two apps that really suck me in. I've deleted them from my phone and only check them through Safari. This has made a huge difference."
> —SIOBHAN

> "I really liked some of these apps, but the weird thing is that I don't miss them at all." —VANESSA

SOCIAL MEDIA AND FOMO

If you delete social media apps from your phone, you are likely going to miss some posts. But instead of directing your FOMO towards what you think you *might* miss if you reduce the amount of time you spend on social media, try focusing on what you are *definitely* missing when you spend time on social media – which is to say, the rest of your life. In other words, missing out on stuff that happens only on your phone is probably a good thing. (Also, if anything big happens, you're still going to hear about it.)

If you're worried about missing invitations to real-life things that are sent via social media, then simply make a point of checking your account from your desktop once or twice a day. Some social media apps also allow you to customise what types of email notifications you'd like to receive – so you can let actual invitations still come through.

Lastly, spending less time on social media will help prevent a different type of FOMO: the jealousy that occurs when you compare your own life to someone else's social media feed. The irony, of course, is that most people's feeds do not accurately represent the proportion of their lives they actually spend skiing/surfing/sitting in hot tubs with models. Also, many people with enormous social media followings are actually *paid* to glamorise their lives. If someone's existence looks too good to be true, it probably is.

COME BACK TO (REAL) LIFE

If you use your phone less, you're going to end up with more time. Unless you have some sense of how you *want* to be spending this reclaimed time, you're likely to feel anxious and possibly a bit depressed – and you'll be at risk of sliding right back into your old habits.

That's why we need to get back in touch with what makes us happy in our offline lives. We're going to start with a few prompts. Just jot down whatever comes to mind.

- I've always loved to:
- I've always wanted to:
- When I was a kid I was fascinated by:
- If I had more time, I would like to:
- Some activities that I know put me into flow are:
- People I would like to spend more time with include:

"Being out in nature brings me joy. Swimming in the sea or a lake makes me really happy. So does spending time with people I love." —DANIELLE

Once you've done this, use your answers to those questions to make a list of several specific fun, off-phone things you could do over the next few days/remainder of our experiment. For example: do a crossword in a café. Go on a day trip. Take a hike. Sign up for a class. Plan a game night. Go to a museum. Draw something. Write a short story. Make a date with a friend. Cook something interesting. Our goal here is to come up with ideas – and plans – for fun things ahead of time, so that when you find yourself with free time, you'll be less likely to reach for your phone.

> *"I've noticed that when I'm really busy and stressed, I get into such a routine that I don't have any fun stuff planned for my downtime, so I just turn to the phone because there aren't readily apparent alternatives."* —VALERIE

DAY 7 (SUNDAY)
GET PHYSICAL

Most of us weren't very good at mind–body integration even before smartphones came into the picture – and with every screen we add to our lives, we're only getting worse. So today, make some time to get back in touch with your body by doing something physical *and enjoyable*. The point is to remember that you are more than a brain sitting on top of a body. And, as a side note, there's strong evidence suggesting that exercise that increases blood flow also helps to strengthen your cognitive control. Some ideas:

- Go for a walk (without your phone). Pay attention to your breath and the feeling of your body as it moves.
- Do yoga.
- Play catch.
- Go to a park and join a game of something.
- Get a massage (get in touch with your body by having someone else get in touch with your body).
- Play one of those video games that require you to jump around a lot.

- If you usually listen to music while you exercise, try turning it off for a bit and tuning in to your body and breath. (Turn the music back on when the sound of your exhausted panting becomes demoralising.)

To practise, put down this book, take a deep breath, and slowly stretch your arms above your head. Bring them back down as you exhale. Notice how it feels.

"I took a dance class and was amazed by how it felt to remember that my body can do things other than just walk and sit. It made me want to get out of my head (and into my body) more often." —ELIZABETH

HEADS UP: GET AN ALARM CLOCK

In the next stage of our break-up, I'm going to ask you to banish your phone from your bedroom. A lot of you are going to breeze on through without doing it. Why? Because you use your phone as your alarm clock.

But think about it: if your phone is your alarm clock, you are guaranteeing that your phone will be the first thing you touch when you get up. So please take a second to prepare for the impending banishment: find – or buy – an alarm clock that is not your phone.

WEEK 2

CHANGING YOUR

HABITS

The difference between technology and slavery is that
slaves are fully aware that they are not free.

—Nassim Nicholas Taleb

IN HIS EXCELLENT BOOK *The Power of Habit*, journalist Charles Duhigg defines a habit as "a choice that we deliberately make at some point, and then stop thinking about, but continue doing, often every day". As he describes it, every habit is a loop made up of three parts:

1. **A cue** (also called a trigger): a situation or an emotion that "tells your brain to go into autopilot mode and let a behaviour unfold".

2. **A response:** the automatic behaviour (that is, the habit).

3. **A reward:** "something that your brain likes that helps it remember 'the habit loop' in the future".

For example: you're feeling bored one day and see your phone on the table (the emotional and physical cue), so you reach for your phone (the response) and are distracted and entertained (the reward). Your brain associates your phone with the alleviation of boredom, and it isn't long before you find yourself reaching for your phone whenever you're faced with even a moment of downtime.

Habits can be helpful: when a task or decision becomes automatic, it frees our brains to think about other things. Imagine how hard it would be to walk home if you had to concentrate on every single step. But habits can also be harmful, and can lead to addictions – for example, if your brain learns to associate the end of a meal with a cigarette.

Regardless of whether they're helpful, harmful or neutral, habits are extremely difficult to break. What's more, once a habit has crossed the line to an addiction, it can be triggered by cues that are so subtle that we don't even notice them. In a 2008 study published in *PLoS ONE*, researchers from the University of Pennsylvania's Center for Studies of Addiction showed images of drug-related cues, such as crack pipes and chunks of cocaine, to twenty-two recovering cocaine addicts as they lay in a brain scanner. Despite the fact that the images were shown for thirty-three milliseconds (that's roughly one-tenth of the time it takes to blink), the reward centres of the subjects' brains lit up in the same way they did when the drug paraphernalia was visible on the screen for a longer, perceptible amount of time.

That's the bad news. The good news is that, while habits can't be eradicated entirely, they can be changed. The easiest way to start is to make adjustments to our lives and environments so that we avoid things that trigger our habits, and to make decisions ahead of time about how we're going to act when we encounter particular situations that we know are likely to trigger us. So that's what we're going to focus on this week.

> *"I feel like my willpower alone should be enough to change/ break my habits. But I know from struggling with previous addictions that willpower alone is insufficient."* —BEN

DAY 8 (MONDAY)
SAY "NO" TO NOTIFICATIONS

Remember the famous experiment where the Russian physiologist Ivan Pavlov conditioned dogs to salivate whenever they heard a bell? He did this by ringing a bell every time he fed them, so that (thanks to dopamine) the dogs began to associate the sound of the bell with the promise of food. Eventually, Pavlov could get the dogs to drool in anticipation any time they heard a bell.

This is exactly what happens to us when we enable push notifications – the alerts that show up on our home and lock screens countless times per day. Notifications use our brains' natural ability to associate cues with rewards (and our anxiety over uncertainty) to get us to compulsively check our phones. Every time you hear or see a notification, you know that there's something new and unpredictable waiting for you – two qualities that we are hardwired to crave.

As a result, not only are notifications nearly impossible to resist, but over time they create a Pavlovian response: we descend into a state of anticipation/anxiety (and therefore distraction) any time we're even *near* our phones. Indeed, the mere presence of a smartphone on the table has been shown to have a negative impact on closeness, connection, and the quality of conversation – not to mention worsen people's performances of tasks that require focused attention. Push notifications can even make us hallucinate. According to a 2017 study at the University of Michigan, more than 80 per cent of college students have experienced "phantom" vibrations or calls.

Notifications are also a very effective way to hijack your attention for profit. "In 2015, users who enabled push notifications launched an app an average of 14.7 times per month, whereas users who did not only launched an app 5.4 times per month," reports Localytics, a marketing and analytics platform, in a company blog post titled "The Year That Push Notifications Grew Up". "In other words, users who opted in to push messages averaged 3x more app launches than those who opted out".

In summary: every ding and vibration from our phones triggers chemical reactions in our brains that pull us away from what we are doing – or the person we are with – and compel us to check our phones, usually for someone else's benefit. Push notifications turn our phones into slot machines, and reinforce the very habit loops that we are trying to change. They are evil and must be destroyed.

DO IT NOW

Go into your phone's notifications settings and **turn off all notifications** except for phone calls and – if you want – messaging apps and your calendar.

You don't have to keep these notifications turned off permanently, but it's important to start by reducing them to a bare minimum. Why? Because then you know that whatever notifications you decide to turn back on are notifications that you actually want to get. (Messaging apps are distracting but they have the option of staying because they represent real-time communication with live human beings; the calendar can stay so that you don't blame me for missing a doctor's appointment.) Then, whenever you install a new app and your phone asks if you would like to enable its notifications, simply say no.

NOTES AND TIPS

- Some people find that they check certain apps more often when their notifications are off than when they're on. If this happens to you, it's fine to re-enable those particular notifications. But I recommend waiting for a day or two before you do so – it's possible that your increased desire to check is a withdrawal symptom that, given time, will fade.

- Notifications don't just take the form of sounds and messages on your lock screen. They also are all those little red bubbles/badges telling you about new messages or things that need to be updated. Turn those off, too.

- When I say "turn off all notifications", I also mean **disabling notifications for email** – including the red bubble and the dings that announce the arrival of new messages. As an email addict myself, I can assure you:

you're not going to forget to check them. (The easiest way to do this is to simply turn off the fetch-new-data setting. This will stop your phone from checking email in the background.)

Speaking of emails, take a moment to go into the settings of your social media accounts, and customise your email notification settings so that you get email alerts only for things you care about, such as invitations. (You'll have to do this from your computer because I made you delete the apps – sorry!) You'll be able to see all these updates when you actually *choose* to log in to your social media accounts; you're just making it less likely that an email check turns into a social media spiral.

"I have really enjoyed having my phone on silent and minimising notifications. It has made a world of difference in making me more present." —KRYSTAL

EMAIL PRO TIP: THE POWER OF VIPS

You may be resisting the idea of turning off your email notifications because there are certain people – like, say, your boss – whose emails you don't want to miss. The solution is to set up a list of Very Important People, and then to tell your phone that you only want to receive notifications for emails from those people.

THE LIFE-CHANGING
MAGIC OF TIDYING APPS

As we talked about in "The Wake-Up", most of the person-alisation options on our phones are meant to increase – not reduce – the amount of time we spend on our devices. So let's personalise our phones with our own interests in mind. We'll start by deciding which apps we actually want to have on our phones.

The first step is to sort your apps based on two criteria: their potential to **steal your attention** (that is, suck you in) and their potential to **improve your daily life** (make your life logistically easier, or bring you pleasure/satisfaction). This should result in (at most) six categories of apps.

1. TOOLS

For example: maps, photos, camera, password manager, ride-sharing, thermostat, security system, banking, weather, music, the actual phone.

These are the apps that improve your life without steal-ing your attention. They are the *only* apps allowed to be on your home screen.

Why? Because they serve a practical purpose without being tempting. They help you accomplish a specific task without any risk that you will be sucked into a black hole.

Note that email, games, shopping sites, and social media all have black hole potential and thus do not get to be on your home screen. I also recommend not letting news apps onto your home page. Internet browsers are a judgment call.

If you find yourself with more apps than can fit on one page, prioritize them according to how often you *want* to be using them. You can relocate the rest into an overflow folder on the same screen or – if you really want to minimize temptation – put *all* of your apps into folders so that their icons become too small to even read. And remember: your home screen does not need to be full.

HOW TO ORGANISE APPS

To move an app, tap and hold its icon and then drag it to its new location (to put it on a different page, drag it past the edge of the screen).

To create a folder, drag one app's icon on top of another app's icon and release. This will create a folder, which you can then rename.

2. JUNK FOOD APPS

For example: social media, news apps, shopping apps, internet browsers, messaging apps, real estate apps, games, email.

These are the apps that are fun or useful in limited quantities, but that are hard to stop using once you start. They sometimes can be life-improving, but they also threaten to suck you in.

The trick is to decide whether they steal your attention more than they improve your life, or if they improve your life more than they threaten to steal your attention. If an app's risks outweigh its benefits, delete it. (If you hesitate, remember that you can always reinstall it.) If your enjoyment of the app outweighs its risk, relocate it to your phone's second screen and hide it in a folder, ideally with a title that reminds you to think before you open it. For most people, email qualifies as a junk food app.

"Dating goes into a subfolder titled 'Ughhhh.'" —DANIEL

UNDECIDED?

Some apps, including most social media and dating apps, can straddle the line between junk food and the next category, slot machine apps. If you're on the fence about which category an app falls into, delete it for a few days and see how it feels.

3. SLOT MACHINE APPS

For example: social media, dating apps, shopping apps, games.

Every app on our phones is a dopamine trigger – but slot machine apps are the worst. These are the apps that don't improve your life *and* steal your attention.

Signs that an app is a slot machine/junk food app:

- You feel a sense of anticipation when you open it.
- You find it hard to stop using it.
- After you use it, you feel disappointed, unsatisfied, or disgusted with yourself.

Slot machine apps suck. Delete them.

WHAT TO DO ABOUT GAMES

If you find games problematic, try this strategy, suggested to me by someone who loves them. First, delete your games. Then, any time you want to play one of them, reinstall it. When you're done playing, delete it again. Repeat as needed. Note: you can also use this technique for dating apps. Just reinstall them when you feel like swiping.

> *"It's too easy to become a slave to a game if it stays on your phone. Most games have no ending, just endlessly new levels that are progressively harder. Better to enjoy it for a moment and let it go."*
> —DUSTIN

4. CLUTTER

For example: the QR reader I installed in 2012 and haven't looked at since.

These are the apps that you never actually use. They don't steal your attention, but they also don't improve your life.

What you do with these apps is likely to reflect your approach towards your real-life junk. Some people will find it easy to recognise their irrelevance and delete them. Other people will hide them in a folder on the third page of their phones and, like overflowing closets, continue to ignore their existence. I will leave it to you to guess which technique I endorse.

5. UTILITY APPS

There are also some apps that serve some practical purpose, but don't improve your daily life enough to be qualified as full-on tools (for example, Find iPhone, the app that communicates with my washing machine via mysterious beeps and then tells me what's wrong with it). Keep these utility apps in a folder on your third page.

> *"Oddly, moving the App Store off my home screen has been lovely. I hate seeing that things need to be updated all the time. It feels like a never-ending to-do list."* —FELICIA

6. THE UNDELETABLES

There are some apps that you simply can't delete because your phone won't let you – which is a total dick move, if you ask me. You can hide them in a folder on your third page, with a title of your choosing.

FOLDERS: A FORCE FOR GOOD

With the possible exception of your home screen, I want you to put your apps into folders even if it means that most of your screen is empty. The point of the folders is not just organisation (though it certainly does scratch a certain OCD itch). The point is to protect yourself from yourself: if you put apps into folders, their icons become so small that when you swipe over to that page, you can't immediately tell which apps are where.

This means that instead of opening an app just because you happen to see its icon (that is, *reacting*), you have to proactively *want* to open the app. This helps promote the habit – which I highly recommend – of launching apps by typing their names into the search bar, rather than by scrolling through your apps and being tempted by whatever else you see along the way. It also prevents the common habit of opening up one app and then getting swept into your personal "app loop" that you mindlessly cycle through every time you pick up your phone.

THE POWER OF GRAYSCALE*

If you've tidied your apps and put them into folders, and *still* find your phone too tempting, try switching your phone's display from colour to grayscale (black and white). It will make your phone look like a Xerox copy of itself – which turns out to be a very unattractive effect.

PHONE HACK

If you have so many apps that the idea of sorting them all seems overwhelming, open your phone's settings and go to the Battery page. You should be able to find a list of all the apps you've opened recently, as well as what percentage of your battery power they've consumed. This will tell you which apps you're using the most – and give you a good starting point.

---

* Not to be confused with *grey*scale, the *Game of Thrones* affliction that leaves the skin stiff and stonelike (though, then again, that is one potential side-effect of spending too much time on your phone).

THE MENU BAR

Most people never think to touch their menu bars – their position at the bottom of the screen makes it seem like they can't be changed. But menu bars are indeed customisable. So let's customise them.

If you haven't already, take your email out of the menu bar and banish it to an interior page, ideally in a folder. If there are other attention-stealing apps in your menu bar, like messages or an internet browser, move them, too.

You can leave those slots empty if you'd like. Alternatively, choose several Tool apps such as the phone or your password manager to which you'd like to have particularly easy access and move them to the menu bar.

YOUR NEW PHONE

By the end of our personalisation process, you should be left with the phone equivalent of a Container Store catalogue. I hope that it will make you feel similarly soothed.

- **Menu bar:** the chosen few
- **Home screen:** tools
- **Second screen:** curated junk food apps, email
- **Third screen:** utilities, undeletables, clutter*
- **Deleted:** slot machine apps, plus every junk food app that sucks you in more often than it serves a purpose or brings you joy

---

* Just go ahead and delete these. You've come this far.

"Tidying my phone and making it seem less cluttered gave me peace – both aesthetically and also in terms of distraction. With only apps that I 'need' on my phone, I'm less likely to open it up and scroll mindlessly." —MICHAEL

DAY 10 (WEDNESDAY)
CHANGE WHERE YOU CHARGE IT

Now that we've reorganised our phones to minimise temptation, we're going to do the same thing for our off-phone environments, starting with one of the biggest problem spots for many people: the bedroom.

Many of us complain about automatically checking our phones first thing in the morning and right before bed at night (and in the middle of the night, for that matter). Well, *of course* we're doing this: we're sleeping within arm's reach of our phones.

The easiest way to break this habit is to make it harder to reach for your phone while you're in bed. And the easiest way to do that is to create a charging station for your phone and other internet-enabled mobile devices that isn't in your bedroom – or, at very least, that's not right next to your bed. (If you haven't already got hold of a non-phone alarm clock, please do so now.)

This does not mean that you *can't* check your phone/internet-enabled devices during these times if you want to, or that you have failed in some way if you find yourself standing alone next to an outlet at 2 a.m., squinting down at your phone's tiny screen. The point is just to change checking your phone in the morning and evening from an automatic habit to a deliberate choice.

So do it now: pick a new charging spot. As soon as you get home – or right now, if you're already there – take the charger from your bedroom and plug it into your new charging station. Then remove all extra chargers from your bedroom and store them in a different room (or, if you live in a studio or dorm room, hide them in a drawer). You are simply a person who does not charge their phone in the room where they sleep. End of story.

- For the best results, the rest of your family should do this as well. All phones should be charged in the same spot, so that it's easy to tell if anyone is cheating. One way to get kids/roommates/partners/parents on board is to get a jar – your "Phone Bank" – and establish a fine for anyone caught cheating. At the same time, mutually agree on fun things you could do together that don't involve phones, such as going to dinner together. Then, when your Phone Bank is full, use the money to have one of those experiences.

- If you encounter resistance, tell your antagonist that you are trying to reduce your smartphone use so that you can be more connected to the people you care about – including them.

- In an ideal world, you wouldn't see your phone at all until you consciously decided to check it. One technique is to charge your phone while you're at your desk (or in class) and then keep it in your bag or coat pocket overnight so that you don't encounter it until you leave the house.

- If you're worried that you'll miss an important call when your phone's in the other room, turn the ringer on. (Just be sure that you've turned off notifications so that it's not constantly dinging at you.) This essentially turns your smartphone into a landline, and makes it possible to move freely around your home/apartment/room without keeping it strapped to your side.

So tell me: where will your phone be sleeping tonight?

"Removing my phone from my room is something I have aspired to for years and finally doing it has improved my sleep significantly. It also prevents me from being overly anxious about ongoing communications (texts and email mostly) by forcing me to allow those conversations to pause. I don't need to respond right away." —DUSTIN

DAY 11 (THURSDAY)
SET YOURSELF UP FOR SUCCESS

Now that we've removed some of the triggers that make us automatically reach for our phones, we're going to add some *new* triggers: things that make it more likely for us to do the things we say we want to do, or that we know that we enjoy. In other words, we're trying to help ourselves transition from a negative goal (using our phones less) to a positive goal: living up to our intentions. We're trying to establish happier, healthier habits.

For example, if you feel the urge to use your phone while driving, your first step might be to keep your phone out of reach while you're in the car (avoid the trigger). Your next step might be to plan some positive alternatives. You could program your favourite stations into your radio, or hit "Play" on a podcast you've been meaning to listen to *before* you head out on the road. One previous text offender put a Post-it note on her dashboard that said, "Sing!"

Some other ideas:

- If you are trying to meditate every morning when you get up, then decide ahead of time how long you'll meditate, and what the focus of your meditation will be. Choose a spot where you will meditate, and make that space as calm and distraction-free as possible.

- If you say you want to read more, pick a particular book or magazine you're interested in, and put it on your bedside table or in your bag or pocket.

- If you want to play more music, take your instrument out of its case and put it somewhere you're going to see it.

- If you want to be less tempted to bring your phone into your bedroom to soothe yourself before sleep, make your bedroom a more soothing place to be in without your phone. Get a nice set of sheets. Hang pictures that calm you. Do something involving lavender.

Please take a second to identify several changes you can make to your environment to make it more likely that you'll do the things you say you want to. Then make those changes.

"I could lay out exercise clothes on the chair in my bedroom the night before so that I am more likely to run/walk right after the kids are out the door." —CHRISTINE

IDENTIFY YOUR TRUE REWARDS

My hope is that by this point in the break-up you've developed some awareness of the rewards behind your habits – what your brain is actually after when you reach for your phone (for example: connection, new information, distraction, alleviation of boredom, escape, a break from the task at hand).

If you're not sure if you've correctly identified the reward, try running an experiment on yourself. For example, if you think you're reaching for your phone out of a desire for distraction, try taking a break in a different way, such as getting a cup of coffee, or chatting with a friend or colleague. If your craving for your phone goes away, you've successfully identified the reward – as well as an alternative way to provide it. If not, test a different hypothesis. Once you've figured out your rewards, you can start thinking of other things you could do – besides grabbing your phone – to achieve the same result.

DAY 12 (FRIDAY)
DOWNLOAD AN APP-BLOCKER

We tend to think about our relationships with our phones as all-or-nothing affairs: if we give ourselves access to one app, then we worry that we'll also be giving ourselves access to all the other tempting apps on our phones.

But it doesn't have to be this way. The solution is simply to download an app-blocker: an app that blocks your access to sites and apps that you tend to get sucked into, while still letting you use the rest of your phone.

The first step is to acknowledge (and get over) the irony of using an app to protect yourself from your apps. The second is to use the app to set up "block lists" of problematic sites and apps, organised into specific categories and contexts. For example, my lists include "The News", "Focused Work", "Extreme Nights", and "Weekend Mornings".

Then, whenever you want undistracted time (or want to use your phone for something without having to worry about temptation), you simply start a session, specifying which block list(s) you want to enable and for how long. (See Recommended Resources, page 169, for specific app-blocker suggestions.)

Some of these apps allow you to schedule sessions in advance – which is a fantastic way to change your habits. (If you want to stop checking social media before bed, you simply block your access to social media before bed.) And some app-blockers come with an added bonus: the ability to block sites and apps *across devices*, meaning that if you've got something blocked on your phone, you can't cheat and look at it on your computer.

App-blockers are particularly useful if you need to use social media apps for work or school. They're also useful any time there's an app that you know is problematic, but that you can't bear to keep off your phone – such as dating apps that don't have browser versions. If you simply *must* have access to these apps, you can use an app-blocker to set a schedule ahead of time so that you have access to them only during certain hours of the day. I personally use my app-blocker to prevent myself from obsessively reading the news: now that I know that I can't access the sites or apps from my phone, I no longer feel as much of an urge to try. (And somehow I don't seem to be any less informed than I was before.)

SET BOUNDARIES

Now that we've established some digital boundaries for ourselves, it's time to get physical.

1. ESTABLISH NO-PHONE ZONES

As the name suggests, a "No-Phone Zone" is a place where you do not use your phone. Full stop. No-Phone Zones are great because they remove the need for decision-making in the moment. They can also help reduce conflict: if everyone knows that phones aren't allowed at the dinner table, then you don't need to have a new argument about it each night.

Take a moment to establish several No-Phone Zones for yourself and, if applicable, your family or roommates. I suggest starting with the dinner table and bedroom: banning phones from the dinner table brings people together, and banning phones from bedroom improves sleep.

The effective date of your No-Phone Zones should be tonight, and these zones should continue to be off-limits for the remainder of our 30-day experiment.

"No phones on the table! I will try to get my husband to do this, too. Part of the reason I end up picking mine up is because he's on his." —ERIN

2. GIVE YOUR PHONE A WAKE-UP TIME

You can also create No-Phone Zones based on time – for example, no checking email after 6 p.m. Since it's the weekend, though, let's focus on the morning instead. Here's what I'd like you to do:

- Assign your phone a wake-up time for tomorrow morning. This should be at least an hour after you get up yourself.

- Choose something restorative or fun that you will do for yourself while your phone sleeps. For example: Reading a book. Playing with your pet. Cooking a nice breakfast.

There are two ways to enforce your phone's wake-up time. The first is to put it on Airplane Mode (or turn it off) and charge it in a place where you won't see your phone at all until its wake-up time. The second method is to use your new app-blocker to enforce your phone's wake-up time. This approach is useful when you want to have access to certain features on your phone but not others – say, you're trying to coordinate breakfast with someone and don't want to miss a call or text, or you're going for a walk and want to be able to use the camera. Simply create a block list with the problematic apps and sites, give it an appealing name (something like "Weekend Break"), and start a session. If your app-blocker has the option, you can even schedule recurring sessions in advance – which is a fantastic way to reclaim weekend mornings for yourself.

"I find that if I don't reach for my phone first thing in the morning, then I tend to have a better relationship with my phone for the rest of the day, too." —JOAN

DAY 14 (SUNDAY)
STOP PHUBBING

Phubbing is short for *phone snubbing*. Having your phone on the table during a meal? That's phubbing. Checking your phone in the middle of a conversation? Phubbing. Texting while you're at a party? Phubbing. These types of behaviours have become so common that we often don't even notice that we're engaging in them. But we are.

You've likely already begun to reduce your phubbing, thanks to all the work you've put in to the breakup so far. But let's make it official: from now until the end of our experiment, please do your best not to phub – starting today, by keeping your phone off the table at meals. (If you've already designated your table as a No-Phone Zone, you are ahead of the game.)

"Checking your phone is like picking your nose: there's nothing wrong with it, but no one should have to watch you do it." —ALEX

PHUBBING RULE OF THUMB

Phones should add to, not subtract from, your interactions.

- Okay to pull out phone: if the involved parties agree that the phone is adding to the interaction – for example, showing a friend your vacation photos.

- Not okay to pull out phone: if you are using your phone to distance yourself from the interaction you are supposedly having (for example, you're bored with the conversation, so you start texting someone else).

WHAT TO DO ABOUT OPP (OTHER PEOPLE'S PHONES)

One of the things that makes phubbing so tricky to deal with is that the less you do it yourself, the more you'll notice when it's being done to you.

Eating with friends, colleagues, and classmates can be particularly difficult because even if you have your own phone tucked away, it's likely that they'll have their own phones out on the table.

When you have guests over to your home, consider asking them to leave their phones in a basket by the door. At first they'll think you're a total weirdo, but by the time they leave, they may consider adopting the same ritual themselves.

If you're out, you can keep your own phone off the table and then make a point of asking your dining companion for permission before you check it – the equivalent of "Do you mind if I take this call?" Chances are that the friend will give you a confused look, as if you have just asked permission to breathe. This is your opportunity to explain that the reason you are asking for permission is that you are trying not to phub people. Not only is this an interesting conversation starter, but it also will make your dining companions feel mildly self-conscious the next time they feel the urge to pull out their own phones.

In the beginning, this can feel pretty forced and manipulative (because, in the beginning, it will be forced and manipulative). But once you get into the habit of keeping your phone off the table, you may begin to ask permission out of a genuine desire to not be rude.

If you're with a close friend, you can turn this into a playful ritual. For example, when something comes up in conversation that we want to check, several of my friends and I regularly use "Permission to use phone?"/ "Permission granted" as an easy way to make sure that we're all on the same page and that no one feels phubbed.

> *"When you're out for dinner with friends and everyone else is on their phones, try taking a photo of them on their devices and then texting it to them with a note saying, 'I miss you!'"*—NATE

IF YOU ARE A PARENT, BOSS, OR TEACHER

It's a bit easier to deal with other people's phones when you're the one in charge. We've already talked about establishing No-Phone Zones at the dinner table as a way to reduce phubbing. Depending on your position, you could also ban phones in meetings or classes.

If you think that going cold turkey will be impossible for your children/colleagues/students, you could offer a one-minute "tech break" in the middle of the meal or class or meeting so that people can check their phones. That's a suggestion from psychologist Larry Rosen, a professor of technology and behaviour who wrote a book called *iDisorder* about how our phones are causing us to exhibit symptoms of psychiatric disorders like ADHD and OCD.

The trickiest thing about setting rules is that *you* have to follow them. Don't be the jerk who tells their kids that they can't check their phones at the dinner table, only to keep yours by your side.

IF YOU'RE A KID AND YOUR PARENTS PHUB YOU

Call them out on it! When it comes to acknowledging their smartphone addictions, parents are the *worst*. They're also particularly vulnerable to feeling guilty about things they might be doing now that will screw you up later. You can make your objection known directly ("Please stop phubbing me") or take a more aggressive approach ("I hope you know that every minute you spend on your phone while we're together is a minute that I'll be spending in therapy").

HOW TO RESPOND TO PHONE CALLS AND TEXTS WHEN YOU'RE WITH OTHER PEOPLE

First step: consider *not* responding. (What's the worst that could happen? We all have a somewhat inflated sense of our own importance.) If you decide that you are going to take a call or engage in a conversation by text while you're around other people, consider leaving the room, even if you're home. It's less rude, and it's also annoying to have to do, which makes it less likely that you will take calls in the middle of meals or start texting under the table.

HOW TO BE REACHED IN AN EMERGENCY

If you are worried that not having your phone on the table in front of you will make you miss a call in an emergency, you can adjust your Do Not Disturb settings to allow phone calls from a select group of contacts. You can do this either by taking the time to create groups of contacts – a process that for some reason often has to be done from a computer – or you can also just put your chosen contacts into your "Favorites" list. Then set your phone to Do Not Disturb, and adjust the Allow Calls From setting to include "Favourites".

Also, it's worth noting that most Do Not Disturb controls include a feature that will override the Do Not Disturb function if you get another call from the same person within three minutes – which is presumably what someone who desperately needed to reach you would do (especially if you tell them about this ahead of time).

WEEK 3

RECLAIMING
YOUR BRAIN

Our ability to maintain our focus in one information patch – whether it be a work project, a homework assignment, or something as simple as watching a television program – has been seriously jeopardized, and we believe that modern technology is a major culprit.

—Adam Gazzaley and Larry Rosen, *The Distracted Mind: Ancient Brains in a High-Tech World*

IN "THE WAKE-UP", we talked about how spending hours a day on our phones has negative effects on our attention spans, memories, creativity, stress levels, and general experience of life.

So now let's work on undoing some of these effects.

Many of this week's exercises are inspired by mindfulness. As you know, we've been practising mindfulness already by noticing when and why we use our phones and how it makes us feel. But we're now going to take this a step further, and explore how we can use more formal mindfulness practices to retrain our brains and strengthen our attention spans.

STOP, BREATHE AND BE

Stop, Breathe and Be is a mindfulness exercise that I learned from Michael Baime, head of the Penn Program for Mindfulness at the University of Pennsylvania. You can use it to remind yourself to pause before reaching for your phone – or to ground yourself any time you're feeling anxious or agitated in general.

Stop, Breathe and Be is just what it sounds like: you stop what you're doing, take a slow, deep breath, and tune in to the details of what you're experiencing in that moment. There are many ways to do this, from noticing the physical sensations in your body to scanning your thoughts and emotions to taking note of your surroundings.

The point of Stop, Breathe and Be is to create another speed bump between your impulses and actions, and to give yourself a moment to reorient yourself so that you can decide what direction you actually want to go. If you're using it as a way to stop yourself from reaching automatically for your phone, try following it with a round of WWW (What For? Why Now? What Else?), described on Day 4, page 89.

Today, I'd like you to do at least two rounds of Stop, Breathe and Be – starting with one right now.

"My body is tense, especially in my chest. It's okay to let myself have this moment, to breathe." —EMILY

"One of the buds on my orchid blossomed. I didn't notice until now." —DARA

DAY 16 (TUESDAY)
PRACTISE PAUSING

Today, we're going to start practising something that's simultaneously simple and hard: being still. We tend to think of stillness as being synonymous with boredom, and it's true that we often use both words to describe the same state of mind. But while the word *boredom* carries with it an element of feeling trapped, stillness offers an opportunity for peace. As Pema Chödrön writes in her book, *When Things Fall Apart: Heart Advice for Difficult Times*: "If we immediately entertain ourselves by talking, by acting, by thinking – if there's never any pause – we will never be able to relax. We will always be speeding through our lives."

Stillness also gives your mind the space it needs to be creative and come up with new ideas. So let's experiment with deliberately making time to be still.

First, identify several situations in which you regularly find yourself reaching for your phone to kill a little bit of time (by "little bit" I mean anywhere from ten seconds to ten minutes). For example: taking the lift, waiting to cross the street, taking a cab, using the bathroom, having lunch.

Next, choose two or three of those situations – ideally ones that you know you'll encounter today – and commit to being still. Tomorrow, choose a few more, and do the same thing. From now through the end of our time together, try to make small doses of stillness a regular part of your day.

There are many ways to be still. Stare at the ceiling. Notice the people around you. Taste what you're eating. Look out of a window at the sky. It doesn't really matter what you do, as long as you don't reach for a distraction.

At first you're likely to feel physically and emotionally twitchy, as if your brain is banging on a door that usually opens, and panicking when it realises that it's locked. But after a few minutes – or even seconds – your brain will tire itself out. It will stop pounding on the door and start noticing the room that it's already in. And who knows? It might decide that it likes it there.

> *"When I notice myself reaching for my phone on the way home just to kill the time because I'm impatient and have nine stops to go, I leave the phone in my bag and just sit there and do nothing. It's seriously so relaxing and it's helping me wind down at the end of the day so that I don't go from the office phone/email to the tube email on phone to home where I feel like I should still be working."* —JANINE

DAY 17 (WEDNESDAY)
EXERCISE YOUR ATTENTION SPAN

Now that we've begun to deliberately practise stillness, our next step is to work on restrengthening our muscles of attention and rebuilding our ability to ignore distractions. It's like any skill: the more you practise sustaining your attention, the better you'll get at it.

Today, we're going to experiment with some informal ways to build an attention-building workout into your day. One way to start is to devote a period of time every day – for example, your walk to work or class – toward actively focusing on something. You could think about a project or problem you're working on professionally or personally. Or you can work on strengthening some mental skill, such as multiplying two-digit numbers in your head. (Don't knock it before you try it.) The idea is to build your capacity for focus by, well, *focusing*.

You can also play around with other informal practices. For example, you could take a "music bath": get comfortable and close your eyes as you listen to a favourite piece of music as closely as you can, trying to pick out each individual instrument. You could write in a journal, or go to a yoga class, or send a handwritten letter to a friend or relative or mentor.

Or, you could do something even more straightforward: read – in print, and with your phone off. Not only can getting lost in a book be a very relaxing and restorative experience, but it's also exactly the type of mental exercise that strengthens our attention spans and encourages deep and creative thought.

Why? Because extracting meaning from symbols requires your brain both to maintain focus on those symbols and to simultaneously ignore everything else going on around you. Over time, regular reading causes physical changes to the brain in areas responsible for reasoning, processing visual signals and even memory.

In other words, learning to read doesn't just enable us to store and retrieve information; it literally changes the way we think. It reorganises our neural circuitry in a way that encourages creativity, problem solving, and insight. And it increases our ability to sustain attention. In fact, many scholars believe that the development of written language was an integral step toward the development of culture. As Maryanne Wolf writes in her fascinating book about reading, *Proust and the Squid*: "New thought came more readily to a brain that had already learned how to rearrange itself to read."

For the rest of our time together, please incorporate at least one attention-building exercise into your daily routine – starting right now.

"I sat in the car and listened – and actually paid attention to – a story on NPR while I was waiting for a store to open. It felt fine. It felt wonderful, actually, to just sit, do nothing, and listen to a story." —JENNY

HOW YOU DO ANYTHING IS HOW YOU DO EVERYTHING

One of my favourite exercises is to practise doing just one thing at a time: choose a chore – such as folding the laundry or chopping onions – and devote your full attention to it. You may be surprised by how changing the way you perform these small tasks affects the way you approach other aspects of your life. There's a saying, "How you do anything is how you do everything." Think about that the next time you brush your teeth.

MEDITATE

As we've discussed, paying attention isn't just about choosing what to focus on. It's also about ignoring everything else. And that second part in particular takes a lot of work – especially given our brains' predispositions toward distraction. As neuroscientist Adam Gazzaley puts it, "ignoring is an active process". It requires our prefrontal cortexes to exert top-down control, suppressing activity in certain brain areas so that the object of our attention stands out. The better we are at ignoring, the better we are at paying attention. And it turns out that being able to ignore distractions is good for our working and long-term memories, too.

Today, we're going to experiment with a formal attention-building practice known as mindfulness meditation, a secularised form of Buddhist meditation that's been proven to reduce anxiety levels, increase cognitive control, and make it easier for you to slip into flow.

In mindfulness meditation, you choose something from your present experience to focus on – for example, your breathing, external sounds, physical sensations, or even the coming and going of thoughts – and then you try to maintain your attention on that one thing for a set period of time, without judging yourself or trying to change anything.

Jon Kabat-Zinn, founder of the Center for Mindfulness at the University of Massachusetts Medical School, calls this a "state of non-doing" – and if that sounds easy, trust me: it's not. Even people whose attention spans have not been weakened by their phones will find that it's nearly impossible to maintain their focus on anything without their minds wandering. Not only is that completely normal, but it is what our minds are built to do. As one of my meditation teachers liked to say, "Your mind wanders because you have a mind."

The trick is not to fight your mind when it wanders. Instead, once you notice that your attention has drifted, gently bring it back without criticising yourself. You're likely to have to do this multiple times during your practice – possibly every few seconds, depending on how quickly you notice that it's happened. And that is totally fine. The very fact that you noticed that your mind has wandered means that you're doing it right.

If you have been using your phone a lot recently, you're likely to find this type of exercise to be particularly difficult. But the harder you find it, the more important it is to do – and the more you do it, the better at it you'll become.

Today, I'd like you to experiment with a brief session of mindfulness meditation. You have two options for how to do so, one of which involves your phone, and one of which does not.

If you don't want to use your phone, just set a timer, close your eyes, and try to train your focus entirely on your breath for five minutes. When your mind wanders – which it will – gently bring your attention back to your breath, over and over and over again. (You can also do this using prayer or mala beads, taking two or three breaths for every bead.)

Your other option is to do a guided meditation using – gasp – the internet or your phone. Yes, I recognise the irony of that suggestion. But as is also true with the app-blocking apps we experimented with earlier, this is a case in which your phone can be an extremely useful tool. There are many excellent online guided meditations and meditation apps, most of which have free versions (see Recommended Resources, page 169, for suggestions).

If you are worried about getting sucked into a phone spiral before, during, or after your meditation, you can use your app-blocker to block access to other apps when you meditate. You can also reduce temptation – and increase the likelihood that you'll actually stick with the practice – by giving your meditation app a prominent spot on your newly redesigned home page.

So please choose one of these options, and try a five- to ten-minute meditation. If you find the experience intriguing, experiment with making a short meditation session part of your daily routine. Keep it up, and by the end of the break-up you'll have two weeks under your belt.

"Now that I've started a regular meditation practice, I've been blown away by the slow but steady increase in my attention span and the decreasing feeling of inadequate-ness and not-getting-stuff-done-ness." —VANESSA

DAY 19 (FRIDAY)
PREPARE FOR YOUR TRIAL SEPARATION

Good news! The break-up part of this process is almost complete. But before we can move on to the final stage – the part where we make up with our phones – there's one more thing we need to do: the twenty-four-hour "Trial Separation". You should already have scheduled this into your calendar, so now it's time to put your money where your mouth is – and put down your phone.

Today, our goal is to prepare. Here's what to do to make your trial separation as easy and rewarding as possible.

IDENTIFY WHAT YOU'RE TAKING A BREAK FROM

We've been talking specifically about taking a break from our smartphones, but I highly recommend not using *any* internet-enabled devices with screens, including tablets, smartwatches, laptops and desktop computers. Voice-activated devices like Alexa are your call. TV and movies, too, though I personally recommend avoiding screens entirely. This experiment is supposed to be dramatic.

TELL PEOPLE WHAT YOU'RE DOING

Inform your parents, friends, roommates, bosses, and anyone else who's likely to try to contact you for the next twenty-four hours. (This is both to help you prepare, and to hold you accountable!)

GET OTHERS ON BOARD

Ideally, everyone in your household should participate in the twenty-four-hour break. It can also be fun to recruit a friend to do it with you.

MAKE PLANS

Schedule enjoyable things you can do (and people you can spend time with) during the time you usually spend on your phone. (See your answers to the questions on Day 6, page 99, for ideas.)

USE HARD-COPY INSTRUCTIONS

If you're going to be driving someplace new, print instructions or write down directions ahead of time. (Yup, for this twenty-four-hour period, you will have to navigate without your phone.) Remember: you can always ask for directions.

GET A PAD OF PAPER OR NOTEBOOK

Use it to make a "To-Phone" list of things that you want to do or look up when your Trial Separation is over. (You may well find that by the time you turn your phone back on, you'll no longer care.)

SET AN AUTOMATED PHONE GREETING

If you feel it's necessary, change your outgoing voicemail to explain what you're doing.

CREATE A PHYSICAL CONTACT LIST

If you have a landline, write down the numbers of people you think you might want to call. There's no restriction on phone calls made on landline phones – they represent live contact with people.

USE CALL FORWARDING

Speaking of landlines: it's possible to have all calls from your smartphone forwarded to your landline. Instructions for how to do so vary by carrier, so do an internet search ahead of time. (For more on landlines – and what to do if you don't have one – see pages 155 and 171.)

SET AN OUT-OF-OFFICE RESPONSE

If you're stressed about not responding to emails, set up an email auto-responder (often called a "vacation reply") that explains what you're doing.

SET AN AUTOMATED TEXT MESSAGE RESPONSE

If you're worried about missing texts, set up a text message auto-responder (see Recommended Resources, page 169). This means that any time someone texts you, they will receive an automatic response that says you're not checking your texts (and, optional, that tells them a different way to get in touch with you). I am a bit obsessed with text message auto-responder. It makes it *much* easier for me to take breaks from my phone. And every time I use one, I get messages from friends asking me how to set one up.

DAYS 20–21 (THE WEEKEND)
YOUR TRIAL SEPARATION

You can do your Trial Separation during any twenty-four-hour period this weekend. Make sure that you've done whatever you need to do to prepare. Then, when the time comes, simply turn off your phone – and whatever other devices you've decided to take a break from – and hide it someplace out of sight. Not Airplane Mode. Totally off.

It can be nice to do a short ritual to mark the transition. I personally like to start my phone breaks at dinner on Friday night: my family and I light a candle, join hands, and take three slow breaths before we eat. It puts us in a different state of mind and sets a nice tone for the rest of the weekend.

WHAT TO EXPECT

Some of you might find the Trial Separation to be less difficult than you feared. But you may also be surprised by how
hard or uncomfortable it is. In addition to their many practical purposes, our phones distract us from our emotions.

Don't be surprised if you feel irritable, impatient or
flooded with a wave of existential malaise. You're detox-
ing. If and when that happens, you can choose to sit with
this discomfort – a great practice, even if it's not that pleasant. Alternatively, you can use your extra time to do one of
your pre-identified activities. (By the way, I was personally
surprised by how hard it was to remember/come up with
things that I enjoy doing – and was very reassured to find
that many of the guinea pigs felt the same way.)

Also, a note on attention: you may find it hard to maintain enough focus to do the things you said you wanted to
do – even if it's just reading an article in a magazine. If that
happens, use it as inspiration to do one of the attention-
building practices that we've been experimenting with.

> *"I thought it would be so hard, but I was just sitting on the
> couch, and said to myself, 'Let's give it a go.' I turned off my
> phone and didn't look back."* —DEB

WHAT TO DO WITH YOURSELF
WHEN YOU DON'T HAVE YOUR PHONE

During your Trial Separation, you can use your newfound
free time – of which there will be a lot – to do whatever you
want. Here are a few suggestions.

WHAT TO DO IN AN EMERGENCY

If you have an emergency, then of course you should use your phone! Don't lie in a pool of your own blood trying to call an ambulance via smoke signals while your phone sits in its charger nearby. Also, if you're nervous about leaving the house without your phone, remember that if something happens, *everyone else around you has a phone.*

Make Room for Serendipity

When you have the internet in your pocket, there is no room for serendipity. Instead, there are correct answers – answers that can be found only via the cross-analyses of hundreds of reviews on multiple websites. It doesn't matter that these reviews were written by strangers with whom you might have nothing in common. The fact that they are on the internet gives them more weight than the suggestions of real-life people around you. Barry Schwartz, psychologist and author of *The Paradox of Choice*, refers to this form of researching as "maximising". Not only is it exhausting, but it can also steal the wonderful feeling of discovery that comes from stumbling across things by accident.*

Your Trial Separation is a perfect opportunity to allow serendipity to re-enter your life. Take a walk in a new

---

* Lest I come across as enlightened, you should know that my husband and I have maximised everything from our dust broom to our choice of garbage bags.

neighbourhood. Try a restaurant you've been curious about. Look at the event listings in your local paper and go to something new. No matter what you do, it's likely to be more memorable than staring at your phone.

> *"In the afternoon, I was walking around a city I don't know well for about three hours and instead of trying to figure out how to maximise my time, I just wandered. I felt even-keeled and unhurried. And I had a lovely time."* —LAUREN

Have a Fleeting Relationship

No, I'm not suggesting you have an affair. A "fleeting relationship" is a brief interaction, often with a stranger, that creates a sense of connection. For example: a pleasant exchange with a waiter, a group cheer at a sports bar, or one of those oddly personal chats that seem to occur between strangers on a plane. You wouldn't think that these interactions would mean much, but actually they can have a surprisingly dramatic effect on how "connected" we feel to society at large. The more time we spend looking down at our phones instead of at the people around us, the fewer of these fleeting relationships we will have. So during your Trial Separation, make a point of having at least one fleeting relationship. Notice if it makes a difference to your mood.

Do Something Fun with Real People

Hopefully this is self-explanatory.

> *"With phones and social media, people talk about how it creates greater connectivity. But on our phones we are physically alone."* —DANIEL

YOUR NEW
RELATIONSHIP

It is easy in the world to live after the world's opinion;
it is easy in solitude to live after our own; but the great
man is he who, in the midst of the crowd, keeps with
perfect sweetness the independence of solitude.

—Ralph Waldo Emerson, "Self-Reliance"

CONGRATULATIONS! The hardest part of your break-up is behind you.

By now you should have a much clearer sense of how you use your phone, how you *want* to use your phone, and how you want to be spending your attention. Our goal this week is to begin to lock in these changes. If we do it right, what started as a break-up will end with a break*through*.

TRIAL SEPARATION RECAP

The first step in our make-up is to reflect on – and learn from – our Trial Separations.

We'll start with a series of open-ended questions called "See/Think/Feel/Wonder". Use them as writing prompts or as conversation starters with anyone who did the Trial Separation with you.

- What did you observe about yourself and your behaviour and emotions during your twenty-four-hour Trial Separation? (That is, what did you **see**?)

   "I saw myself interacting with others more. Because I didn't have my phone to turn to, I turned to those I was around and engaged in discussion. Once, when I needed a break, I sat down on a bench and meditated for a few minutes instead of reaching for my phone. I felt even-keeled during the twenty-four hours, balanced." —BEN

- What do these observations make you **think** about? When you reflect back on the experience, what thoughts come into your mind?

   "It made me think that I've been cheating myself out of fully experiencing things." —KRYSTAL

- Now that you've made it through the Trial Separation, how do you **feel** about your phone itself, as well as your relationship with it?

   "I feel like the time away from the phone made me realise how unnecessary it is during certain periods of the day." —KATIE

"I feel much more grateful for the phone now than I was before, as the times I use it are more purposeful and enjoyable." —BETH

- Now that you've completed the Trial Separation and begun to deeply observe your relationship with your phone, what do you **wonder**? What questions do you have? What do you want to know more about? What would you like to investigate further or look into more?

"I wonder what would happen if I just reverted back to a flip phone. I've got a fusillade of old flip phones sitting in dresser drawers. Why not slip my SIM card into one for a week and give it the old college try?" —SANDY

Once you've seen/thought/felt/wondered, consider these questions:

- What was the hardest part?

"Just a few hours without my phone left me feeling lonely and almost depressed. I was with friends, but they were all on their phones throughout the day, which made it difficult in those moments." —DANIEL

- What was the best part?

"The best part was realising that I'm not a total addict. It's almost like when your spouse takes a trip and you realise, 'Oh, I'm still a whole, individual person. I know how to do all these chores my partner usually takes care of, and I can also entertain myself quite capably.' It's like getting back in touch with your identity and finding, reassuringly, that it's still there." —VANESSA

- What surprised you?

  "When I went back on to social media (which sadly I was quite excited to do) there was little on there of interest. I didn't miss anything." —SIOBHAN

- What did you learn from the experience that you can use once your official break-up is over?

  "I need to 'put the phone in its place' more often." —JESSICA

DAY 23 (TUESDAY)
PHAST

Just as intermittent fasting has been shown to be good for our physical health, regular short phone fasts – what I call "phasts" – are essential for our emotional and intellectual health. As you well know, being constantly tethered to our phones exhausts our brains; they need regular phone-free time to recover and rejuvenate. And as is also true with other potentially addictive behaviors, it's important to take a break once in a while just to prove that you can.

There are many ways to phast – and they don't have to be twenty-four hours long. You could continue the practice of turning your phone off when you go to bed on Friday and giving it a Saturday "wake-up" time that's several hours after your own – and use your phone-free mornings to do something nourishing for yourself. You could choose an activity every weekend that you will do without your phone, such as a hike. You could force yourself to take a break from social media by having someone temporarily change your password for you (for example, a friend or your partner).

Whatever you do, remember that the point is not to punish yourself; it's to make yourself feel good. In other words, don't ask yourself, "When could I force myself to take a break from my phone?" Instead, ask yourself, "When would I *like* to take a break from my phone?"

With that in mind, please identify a time today – anywhere between a half hour and an hour will do – when you will leave your phone behind or turn it off entirely. Choose a time when the idea of leaving your phone sounds pleasant. For example: when you're walking your dog, when you're taking a lunch break, or when you're having dinner. Then continue to experiment with these short phasts from now through the end of your break-up. The more regularly you phast, the less you will be drawn toward your phone during the rest of your day.

> *"I went out to dinner with my wife and left my phone at home. It was great! I've continued to leave it behind when going on walks, or just stepping out for a bit. She has been doing the same, so we've been able to connect." —* CRYSTAL

DAY 24 (WEDNESDAY)
MANAGE YOUR INVITATIONS

One of the hardest parts about changing your relationship with your phone is having to constantly say no to invitations sent by your own brain. For example:

"Oh hi. I see that you just woke up. Want to look at your phone to see if anyone messaged you while you were sleeping?"

"It looks like you might be about to try to meditate. How about we just check social media for a second first?"

"This date is boring. Let's excuse ourselves to use the bathroom and then text someone else from the toilet."

We've already done a lot of work on managing our phone-related invitations and making proactive decisions about how we *want* to spend our time and attention, rather than just reacting to our phones. Like many of the things we've been experimenting with, this practice – which, as you know, is rooted in mindfulness – can be extremely useful in the rest of your life as well. Today, let's try expanding the way we use it: try to notice some of the invitations – both phone- and non-phone-related – that your brain is sending. Then make a conscious decision about how you want to respond.

For example, if someone cuts you off in traffic, don't immediately express yourself through hand gestures and choice obscenities. Instead, pause. Stop, breathe, and be. Notice what your brain is inviting you to do. Consider possible alternatives. Then decide how you actually want to react.

"When I reach for my phone, I pause and ask myself, 'Why are you reaching for your phone?' Most of the time, I realise that I was just reaching for it out of habit and the desire for distraction, and I put the phone down without looking at it. It's a great feeling." —BETH

CLEAN UP THE REST
OF YOUR DIGITAL LIFE

Today, we're going to continue to tidy up other parts of our digital lives. We've already talked about text messages, dating and games, app-blockers and password managers, so now let's focus on . . .

EMAIL

You get too many, and most are unimportant.

1. Unsubscribe! For the next week, take a moment to unsubscribe to any email you receive from a list you don't want to be on. Or, if that sounds too complicated, do an internet search for "apps that automatically unsubscribe you from email" – and install one.

2. Save yourself from the tyranny of your inbox. Despite what you've trained yourself to believe, you do not actually have to respond immediately to every message in your inbox. Nor do you even have to see them when they arrive. You can do this in a number of different ways, including setting an app-blocker to give you access to your email inbox only during certain times of day, and/or installing a plug-in for your particular browser and email client (such as Chrome and Gmail) that gives you control over how many times you see your inbox, and for how long. I've been using one of these plug-ins to stay focused while writing this book, and it has been a game changer.

3. Use folders to keep yourself sane. Create a "Needs Response" folder to store messages that actually require a response (you could even sort them by importance) so that when you *do* look at your email, you don't feel overwhelmed by the sight of your entire inbox.

4. Set up a commerce email account. In other words, create a new email address for yourself that you will use when you buy things. This is a way of keeping unwanted spam email out of your primary inbox while still finding out about sales.

5. Set up a VIP list of people whose emails you don't want to miss. (See page 107 for details.) Ignore everyone else. Kidding/not kidding.

6. When you're on holiday, avoid the dreaded email pileup upon your return by creating a new email account along the lines of "[Your Name]_Important." Then set an auto-responder that says not just that you are on holiday and won't be checking emails, but that you won't be reading the emails that accumulate while you're away. Give the name of someone to contact if people need immediate help, and say that if people *really* want to talk to you upon your return, they should resend the message to the aforementioned "important" email address, and that you will respond when you're back. You will be amazed by how few people actually take you up on this. (This is inspired by a German company, Daimler, which automatically deletes employees' incoming emails while they're on holiday and tells senders whom to contact if they need immediate help.) Alternatively, download Thrive Away (thriveglobal.com/apps), an app that

automatically deletes new emails and sends an auto-response telling people when you'll be back in the office.

SOCIAL MEDIA

Ideally, you no longer have social media apps on your phone. But regardless, take a moment to prune your accounts. Unfollow people you don't care about or whose posts make you feel bad. Create lists of people based on their roles in your life (such as friends, family, colleagues, vague acquaintances) so that when you share a photo of yourself on vacation, you can specify which group of people will see it. If you use social media for your job, consider making a separate professional account. Add something to your profile that indicates how often you'll be checking it. And if you haven't already, explore the depths of your social media account settings. There are a lot more options than most of us realise.

DRIVING

Take advantage of automatic drive modes that disable your phone when you reach a certain speed. (Do an internet search for "drive mode" and your phone model/carrier.)

LINKED ACCOUNTS

A lot of sites now give you the option of logging in using your social media account (such as logging in to Spotify using your Facebook credentials). Do not take them up on this option! And if you've already linked your accounts, take the time to begin to separate them (by creating playlists that are independent of your Facebook account, for instance).

"These are the types of things that you know you should do, but which you never seem to get around to. Now that I've finally done them, I'm amazed by how big of an impact they've had on my overall stress levels and sense of control." —EDWIN

DAY 26 (FRIDAY)
CHECK YOUR CHECKING

Here's a great way to catch yourself when you're about to check your phone. Whenever you notice that you're itching to check something – email, social media, text messages, the news, whatever – ask yourself some simple questions: what's the best thing that could happen as a result of your checking? What's the best email you could receive? The best piece of news? The best notification? What's the best emotion that you could experience?

Then ask yourself: what is the likelihood that this will actually happen?

Spoiler alert: your chances are low. Very low. I'm willing to bet that if you were to reach for your phone right now, you would not find a note from a headhunter offering you your dream job, news that makes you feel great, or an out-of-the-blue invitation to dinner from an attractive stranger.

Far more likely is that you're going to see something that upsets you or stresses you out. Once you realise how unlikely your best-case scenario is to happen, it becomes a lot easier to stop checking your phone.

"The more I reach for my phone out of a desire to feel good, the worse it makes me feel." —DAVID

USE OTHER PEOPLE'S CHECKING TO CHECK YOUR CHECKING

The more you pay attention to your own phone habits, the more you're going to notice how often other people are on their phones. You'll see people crossing busy intersections with their eyes glued to their phones. Families that go out to eat together and then spend the meal silently staring at their devices. Subway cars full of faces lit by that familiar blue glow.

Pick a habit that you've been trying to establish, and see if you can use the sight of people on their phones as your cue.

> *"Seeing people in the lift checking their phones used to make me check mine. But now, when I see the person next to me start reaching for his pockets, I use it as a cue to take a deep breath and ask myself what I want to pay attention to in that moment. Unsurprisingly, it's usually not my phone."* —PETER

DAY 27 (SATURDAY)
DIGITAL SABBATH LIFE HACKS

Despite their initial apprehension, many people end up finding the twenty-four-hour break from their phones so rewarding that they decide they'd like to turn the Trial Separation into a regular Digital Sabbath. This doesn't need to happen every weekend; even once a month will go a long way towards inoculating you against compulsively reaching for your phone. Nor do you necessarily need to take a break from *all* of your devices or shut them off completely. The point, as always, is to personalise your experience.

If you're interested in this idea, feel free to use this weekend to experiment with another break. (If you're not, use this weekend to further solidify some of the other habits you've been working on.) Here are some suggestions for how to make it easier to take regular Digital Sabbaths.

UNTANGLE YOUR DEVICES

One of the best things about smartphones – that they serve so many purposes – is also the worst: you pull out your phone to listen to a podcast before bed, and end up spending an hour reading the news. One solution is to invest in separate devices. By now, you should already have a separate alarm clock. Depending on your habits, you might also want to consider getting a separate e-reader or music player or even a digital camera. Or, alternatively . . .

CREATE A "HOUSE PHONE"

Instead of tossing or recycling your old phone when you upgrade, keep it as a pared-down "house phone" that can be used only as a tool: delete all the apps (including the internet browser!) except for the camera, music, timer, calculator, and other purely tool-like functions, such as controlling your thermostat or security alarm. This will turn your phone from a temptation into a remote control. And as long as you have wireless internet, it doesn't require a service plan.

Don't have an old phone? You can buy a used one from eBay. Also, iPods are internet-enabled and can serve the same purpose. The trick is just to be very selective about which apps you install.

USE YOUR PHONE'S SUSPENSION MODES

Put your phone on Airplane Mode – or enable Do Not Disturb – more often. This is yet another "speed bump" that will prevent you from mindlessly checking things on your phone. And speaking of Do Not Disturb . . .

CUSTOMISE YOUR DO NOT DISTURB SETTINGS

Preselect the people whose calls you actually want to receive. This makes it possible to take a break from your phone without worrying that you'll miss an emergency phone call.

DOWNLOAD MAPS AHEAD OF TIME

Did you know that you can download maps of areas that you use frequently so that you still have access to them while you're offline? This is not helpful if you're taking a total break from your phone. But if you want to minimise your phone use *and not get lost*, this is a great option.

GET A LANDLINE

You could always pony up and actually pay for separate phone service. Or if you like the idea of having a landline but don't want to pay for one, get a phone that works over the internet (the technical term is *VoIP*, short for *voice over internet protocol*). This has made it much easier for us to take breaks from our phones without worrying about missing an important call: before we turn off our phones, we can change the settings so that all calls get forwarded to our landline.

Another option, mentioned earlier, is to get in the habit of leaving your phone by the door, blocking all apps except the phone, and turning on the ringer. That essentially turns your smartphone into a landline and ensures that you won't miss any important calls while you're taking a break.

DOWNGRADE TO A "DUMBPHONE"

Dramatic, yes, but why not? You can always go back to your smartphone if it doesn't work out.

DON'T BE AFRAID TO EXPERIMENT

When it comes to establishing a healthy relationship with your phone, there are no rules. Experiment with different ideas and adopt the habits that feel right for you.

DAY 28 (SUNDAY)
THE SEVEN PHONE HABITS OF HIGHLY EFFECTIVE PEOPLE

You've just put a lot of effort into establishing the foundations of a healthy relationship with your phone. But sticking with this new relationship will be difficult. Not only are wireless-enabled mobile devices (WMDs) like smartphones here to stay, but with every new generation, they're also likely to become even harder to put down.

In order to stick to our intentions, it's essential to have a plan. Please come up with your own personalised descriptions for the following seven habits about how you interact with your phone and other WMDs. (Don't be surprised if their effects spread into other areas of your life as well.)

1. I HAVE HEALTHY PHONE ROUTINES

A lot of the changes we've made to our routines (for example, keeping our phones out of our bedrooms) have the *potential* to become habits – but since they're not yet automatic these changes are still pretty fragile.

In order to become true habits, these new behaviours need to become second nature so that we do them without thought. The best way to accomplish this is to make decisions ahead of time about how we want to act in particular situations, so that when we encounter these situations, we follow our new, healthy habits without having to think.

For example:

- Where do you charge your phone?
- At what time do you put it away for the night?
- When do you check it for the first time in the morning? (This can be a time or a situation – for example, "I don't check until I get to the office." You could also have different times for weekdays and weekends.)
- Where do you keep your phone while you're at work?
- Where do you keep your phone while you're at home?
- Where do you keep your phone at meals?
- Where do you carry your phone?
- What do you use your phone for? (For example: practical purposes like navigating, social purposes like

calling and texting, or educational and entertainment purposes such as listening to podcasts.)

- What are the situations in which you have decided that you *don't* use your phone? In the lift, waiting in a queue, or when you're bored or feeling socially awkward?

- Which apps are tools that enrich or simplify your life?

- Which apps do you know are dangerous/the most likely to suck you in? This can be a particularly useful question to answer because it limits what you have to worry about. If you know you've got three apps on your phone that tend to steal your attention, then you can put yourself on high alert when you use those particular apps – and not worry as much about the other things you do on your phone. (Or you could delete those three apps. Just saying.)

- Based on your answer to the previous question, which apps/websites do you block – and when?

2. I HAVE MANNERS, AND I KNOW HOW TO USE THEM

Where do you keep your phone – and how do you interact with it – when you are

- Spending time with people?

- Watching a movie or television show?

- Having a meal?

- Driving a car?

- In classes, lectures, or meetings?

It's also worth thinking about how you'd like *other* people to interact with their phones when you spend time together and how you will request that they do so. (See pages 124 for specific suggestions.)

> "Having a meal: phone totally out of sight.
>
> Driving a car: away. No question.
>
> Classes and lectures: away and muted out of respect for classmates and teachers." —DOUG

3. I CUT MYSELF A BREAK

I mean this in two ways. First, it's important to cut yourself a break if and when you slip back into old habits. This happens to everyone. The less time we spend beating ourselves up, the faster we'll be able to get back on track.

Second, you may want to actually give yourself permission to scroll mindlessly through your phone during a particular time of day (in other words, to use your phone to take a break). Allowing yourself regular guilt-free phone time will help you avoid bingeing and make it much easier to stick to your overall goals long term.

Also, given the effects our phones have had on our attention spans, you may *need* to schedule regular phone time for yourself when you're trying to work on your ability to focus. Start small – maybe you concentrate for ten minutes and then give yourself one minute on your phone – and then build up to longer durations of focus.

If you're worried that a half hour of free phone time will quickly become two hours, then use an app-blocker to schedule sessions for yourself in advance.

Describe your plans for how and when you will give yourself free phone time.

"I really look forward to the moment after both kids are in bed, where I can sink into the sofa with my phone. The trick is just not to let it slip out of control." —CHRISTINE

PERFECTION ISN'T THE POINT

This seems like a good place to point out that if you've gone through this entire break-up, and your relationship with your phone still doesn't feel perfect, don't worry: it's not supposed to. In a sense, our phones – both our relationships with them and the physical devices themselves – are reminders that everything in life is constantly changing and that fluctuations are inevitable. Some days, we will feel good; on others, we won't. And that's okay. As long as we're cultivating self-awareness, we're on the right track.

"It's not like these changes have unlocked an extra twenty-four hours in the day for me during which I've suddenly become the perfect mother, spouse, recreational athlete, and world-class writer. Rather, with fewer clickable distractions, I feel confident that I am doing the most with the time I do have." —VANESSA

4. I PHAST

By now, we've experimented with a lot of different ways to take breaks from our phones. Now's the time to put our intentions down in writing. How and when will you phast?

> *"I'm sticking with no phones when I travel, and after I arrive. In other words, if I go camping this weekend, I use the phone to get there, but then I disconnect once I'm there until it's time to get on the road again."* —DUSTIN

5. I HAVE A LIFE

If we don't have predefined ways to pass the time (or, dare I say, *have fun*) without our phones, then we're much more likely to slip back into our old habits. So take a moment to write a list of some non-phone-related activities that bring you joy or satisfaction, and what you will do to incorporate those activities regularly into your life. For example:

- I enjoy playing guitar – so I will continue to take guitar lessons, and will set aside time every weekend to practice.

- I enjoy staying in touch with people I care about – so when I find myself with twenty to thirty minutes of downtime, I will use my phone to call a friend or family member.

> *"I'd like to have a monthly 'phoneless' dinner party where all my friends and I put our phones in a bin at the start of dinner and we don't use [them] again until we leave."* —DANIEL

6. I PRACTISE PAUSING

Why do *you* think it is important to practice stillness? What will you do when you find yourself with a minute of down-time? Half an hour? Several hours?

> *"When I'm waiting on a tube platform and want to feel less impatient, I will drink a sip of water and breathe deeply."* —LAUREN

7. I EXERCISE MY ATTENTION

In order to undo the damage caused by the cumulative hours we spend on our phones, we need to restrengthen our attention spans – and engage in regular exercise (both mental and physical) to keep our brains in shape. Identify several attention-building exercises that you would like to habitually practice, or that you are already practising and would like to continue.

> *"I will continue to incorporate a fifteen-minute meditation practice into my morning routine three times a week."* —JOHN

> *"I will make a point of trying to do just one thing at a time."* —JULIA

KEEP YOURSELF ON TRACK

We've got two more official days of our break-up; after tomorrow, you're going to be on your own. One of the most effective ways to keep your new relationship on track is to schedule a regular check-in with yourself.

So please pull out your calendar – yes, it's fine if this is on your phone – and create a monthly reminder to check in with yourself. Questions you could ask yourself:

- What parts of your relationship with your phone are going well?

- What things about your relationship with your phone do you want to change? What's one thing you could do to start?

- What are you doing – or could do – to strengthen your focus?

- What are your goals for the next 30 days?

- What fun plans could you make to spend time with people you care about?

- Have you reinstalled any of the apps that you previously deleted, let your phone back into your bedroom, or turned notifications back on? If so, does it feel like the right decision? (No judgment.)

- What do you want to pay attention to in your life?

"Nothing has been reinstalled since it was deleted, phone still sleeps in the kitchen, and I have definitely not turned notifications back on. It feels great, and has made a huge difference." —DARA

CONGRATULATIONS!

You made it. You have officially broken up with your phone and started a new relationship with it – a relationship that I hope makes you feel good.

Thanks to all of your effort, you now have a clear view of how your phone makes your life better. You're aware of how and when it makes you feel bad. You've changed some of your old habits and you've created new ones – and as a result, your phone has gone from being your boss to being a tool. You have joined the growing ranks of people who have taken back their lives from their phones.

In short, you've given yourself an enormous gift. And that's why, for the final exercise of our break-up, I'd like you to give yourself some love. With the recognition that no relationship is perfect, please write a note to yourself describing what you are proud of for accomplishing over the course of this break-up. How have you changed? How do you feel about what you've done?

Some prompts, in case you're stuck:

- I used to think my phone ... Now I think ...
- I've learned that ...
- I'm happy to know that ...
- I'm proud of myself for ...

Once you've written your message, compare it to the note that you wrote yourself at the beginning of the break-up. Take a moment to give yourself credit for what you have accomplished.

"I am getting better about sitting still for a moment. Just a moment. Pausing. Last night, my husband and I sat on the roof and watched a bird. I realised how much forward momentum there is in life. How my instinct was to get up and go make dinner. But when I paused, the forward momentum slowed down." —GALEN

"Remember 30 days ago when you were scared of giving up control of your phone? Well, I think you've learned a valuable lesson. In relinquishing control of the thing that was actually the thing in control, you've also gained more memories. By putting down your phone around family, you learned how much longer and more deliberate time spent with loved ones can feel. By putting down your phone at night and first thing in the morning, you learned that you never once missed a work email that could make or break your work life the following morning. By leaving your phone at home on walks around the neighbourhood, you got to notice more things about the neighbourhood you've lived in for four years – including some amazing restaurants you found by walking [past them] instead of Yelping for hours. By hiding your phone during movies, you had to struggle to figure out who that guy was and what other movies he was in without distracting yourself from the plot and bumming out your fiancé, who really wanted you to watch that movie. Maybe you still feel like your brain needs some serious droll scroll every once in a while, and that's not bad, just cut it off after maybe five cookie-icing videos instead of twenty-five. You know your limits now and that's cool." —JANINE

EPILOGUE

It's now been more than two years since I decided to break up with my own phone, and I'm amazed by how much the experience continues to enrich my daily life.

Today, I still carry my phone with me nearly everywhere, and I use it to take photos, listen to music, navigate, manage logistics, stay connected, and, yes, to indulge in mindless distraction. I appreciate my phone, and am grateful for it.

But I also remain constantly on guard. My research has convinced me that this is not a trivial issue; our phones are having serious effects on our relationships, our brains (especially young ones), and the way we interact with the world. They are designed to addict us – and from what we know so far, the consequences of this mass addiction don't look good. Just take a look around you. Phones are changing the experience of being human.

We need to start having conversations – both individually and as a society – about what we actually want our relationships with our devices to be. And we need to demand that tech companies stop surveilling and "brain-hacking" us and live up to their ostensible missions to do good.

These days, my husband and I still take Digital Sabbaths whenever our schedules allow it. But I also find that I can curb my use without going cold turkey. Like a former smoker who's now repulsed by the idea of smoking, I associate spending time on my phone with feeling bad – which makes me want to spend as little time on it as possible.

Not only has this helped me rebuild my ability to focus, but I've also discovered that reducing my screen time (and increasing the time I spend on offline pursuits) is an easy way to make myself feel more fulfilled. And I've learned that, just as light will fade a photograph, spending too much time on my phone was sapping color from my experiences. The more I pay attention to the actual world around me, the more vividness returns.

We have less time in life than we realise – but we also have more time than we think. Reclaim the hours you spend on your screens, and you'll find that your possibilities expand. Maybe you *do* have time for that class, or book, or dinner. Maybe you *can* spend more time with that friend. Maybe there *is* a way for you to take that trip. The key is to keep asking yourself the same question, again and again and again: this is your life – what do you want to pay attention to?

ACKNOWLEDGMENTS

Thank you to my agent, Jay Mandel at WME, and my editor at Ten Speed, Lisa Westmoreland, for sharing my belief that we all have the power to create healthier relationships with our devices. And a huge shout-out to my guinea pigs: I so appreciate the time you took to participate in this experiment and share your feedback. I have no doubt that your insights will change people's lives, and I hope that you'll continue to stay in touch.

Thank you to my amazing "foreign agent", Janine Kamouh at WME, for sharing my proposal with an international audience, and to all the editors who will be helping incite break-ups around the world (and a special thanks to the UK team for their ideas and designs). Thanks also to my publicist and spreadsheet guru Daniel Wikey, production manager Heather Porter and designer Lizzie Allen for transforming a bunch of words on a screen into something that people might actually put down their phones to read.

Thank you to my family for their unwavering support; to Marilyn Frank, Galen Born, Felicia Caviezel, Christie Aschwanden and Carl Bailik for their wisdom and encouragement; and to Vanessa Gregory and Josh Berezin for their editing prowess. Last, but certainly not least, thank you, Peter and Clara. You are what I want to pay attention to.

RECOMMENDED RESOURCES

Given the speed of technology, there may well be better options by the time this book comes out. For more resources and ideas, please visit howtobreakupwithyourphone.com.

PHONE-USAGE TRACKING APPS

My current favourites are Moment for iPhone and (OFFTIME) for Android. (Note that some of these tracking apps require you to let the app track your location. This isn't for a creepy reason; it's how the app knows when you're using your phone.) You also may want to check out RescueTime, which tracks the time you spend on various websites.

APP-BLOCKING APPS

At the moment, my favourite app-blockers are Freedom (for Apple and Windows products) and (OFFTIME) (for Android). The Freedom app allows you to block apps and sites across your devices, and its paid version is well worth it, because it lets you schedule recurring sessions in advance.

MEDITATION APPS, WEBSITES, AND BOOKS

My favourite app for beginners is Headspace. In its free version, Headspace offers a series of ten-minute guided meditations designed to help people establish their own regular practices – and is an easy way to experiment with meditation to see if it's something you're interested in. I also really like Insight Timer and The Mindfulness App.

As for guided meditations offered online, I recommend that beginners search for "Free Guided Meditation UCLA" and start with the five-minute "breathing meditation." The University of California, Los Angeles, also offers mindfulness-based stress reduction (MBSR) courses that you can take online.

If you're looking to spend your newly strengthened attention span on a book about mindfulness, check out Jon Kabat-Zinn's classic, *Full Catastrophe Living: Using the Wisdom of Your Body and Mind to Face Stress, Pain, and Illness* (Random House, 2013).

If you want something simpler and shorter, you might like a guided mindfulness journal that I wrote, called (appropriately enough) *Mindfulness: A Journal* (Clarkson Potter, 2016). It's aimed toward demystifying mindfulness and helping people establish their own practices.

For practical, tech-focused suggestions, I also recommend David Levy's *Mindful Tech: How to Bring Balance to Our Digital Lives* (Yale University Press, 2016) and Nancy Collier's *The Power of Off: The Mindful Way to Stay Sane in a Virtual World* (Sounds True, 2016).

KIDS AND PHONES

I highly recommend Victoria Dunckley's book, *Reset Your Child's Brain: A Four-Week Plan to End Meltdowns, Raise Grades, and Boost Social Skills by Reversing the Effects of*

Electronic Screen Time (New World Library, 2015), as well as Nicholas Kardaras's *Glow Kids: How Screen Addiction Is Hijacking Our Kids – and How to Break the Trance* (St. Martin's Griffin, 2016).

Common Sense Media (commonsensemedia.org) is a non-profit organisation geared toward helping families establish healthy relationships with media of all kinds. It has a lot of useful articles, reviews, and tips.

There are no official UK guidelines on kids and screen time, but the American Academy of Paediatrics sets guidelines. Their latest recommendations include no screen time for kids under eighteen months (except videochatting), less than an hour a day of high-quality programming for kids up to five years old, and consistent limits for kids over six. The AAP also offers a tool to help families set a "media plan" – visit HealthyChildren.org/MediaUsePlan for details.

If you want to be able to keep track of your kid's location (and call them) but don't want them to have a smartphone (aka access to the entire internet), do an internet search for "GPS tracking watches".

HOW TO SET A TEXT AUTO-RESPONDER

Starting with iOS 11, Apple offers a Do Not Disturb While Driving option that you can use to automatically respond to text messages. Technically, it's designed to prevent you from texting while driving, but you can also use it any time you want to take a break from your phone.

At the moment, the best solution for Android users is to download a third-party app, such as (OFFTIME) or SMS

Auto Reply Text Message, or a provider-specific app such as Verizon's Message +.

WHAT TO GET IF YOU DON'T HAVE A LANDLINE

Get a phone that works over the internet (technically referred to as VoIP, short for *voice over internet protocol*). My husband and I have an Ooma and are very happy with it.

HOW TO SCHEDULE SOCIAL MEDIA POSTS

HootSuite allows you to schedule posts in advance and have them published across multiple platforms. It allows you to appear to be frequently posting when you're actually not.

HOW TO SCHEDULE THINGS
WITHOUT ENDLESS EMAIL CHAINS

Use Doodle or Calendly. Doodle is a group-polling site that lets you propose specific dates and times to a large number of people and have them respond with their availability, which will show up as a red or green *x*. Just pick the time slot with the most green in it.

Calendly allows you to create a personal schedule of times you have available for meetings, interviews, and so on. Then, instead of going back and forth with someone, you simply direct them toward your Calendly page and ask them to select a time that works for them.

WHAT TO DO IF EMAIL CONTROLS YOUR LIFE

Here are some suggestions in addition to those in "Clean Up the Rest of Your Digital Life" on page 149 and the holiday tips on page 150.

Available for both Gmail and Outlook, Boomerang is an extension that allows you to preschedule responses and have certain messages "boomeranged" back at you at times when they're relevant. It also has a great feature called "Inbox Pause" that allows you to choose when you want to be shown new messages, as opposed to being alerted to each message as it comes in.

My favourite for Gmail/Chrome is "Inbox When Ready", which takes away the numbers that tell you how many messages are waiting for you, and hides your inbox unless you explicitly say you want to see it (this allows you to compose new messages or search for old ones without getting distracted by your inbox). It also allows you to set a time limit for how many minutes you want to spend looking at your inbox each day.

HOW TO DOWNGRADE TO A DUMBPHONE WITHOUT ACTUALLY DOWNGRADING TO A DUMBPHONE

Get a forwarding device, such as the Light Phone. Roughly the size of a credit card, the Light Phone can't do anything but make and receive calls. The Light Phone doesn't require you to give up your smartphone or to get a second phone number. Instead, you simply forward your calls to it when you want to leave the house without your smartphone (or want to take a break from it).

How to Share Your Ideas, Experiences, and Recommendations

Email me using the form on howtobreakupwithyourphone.com. I'd love to hear from you.

NOTES

Page 3, **The Smartphone Compulsion Test:** Available on the website for the Center for Internet and Technology Addiction: virtual-addiction.com/smartphone-compulsion-test.

Page 6, **33 times per day:** Deloitte, *2017 Global Mobile Consumer Survey: UK Edition; Consumer and business usage patterns* (2017): 4, www.deloitte.co.uk/mobileuk/assets/img/download/global-mobile-consumer-survey-2017_uk-cut.pdf

Page 6, **2 hours a day:** Hacker Noon, "How Much Time Do People Spend on Their Mobile Phones in 2017?" May 9, 2017, hackernoon.com/how-much-time-do-people-spend-on-their-mobile-phones-in-2017-e5f90a0b10a6.

Page 6, **More than a third of UK adults:** Deloitte, *2017 Global Mobile Consumer Survey, i.*

Page 6, **Among teenagers:** Deloitte, *2017 Global Mobile Consumer Survey,* 10.

Page 6, **repetitive strain injuries:** Deepak Sharan et al., "Musculoskeletal Disorders of the Upper Extremities Due to Extensive Usage of Hand-Held Devices," *Annals of Occupational and Environmental Medicine* 26 (August 2014), doi.org/10.1186/s40557-014-0022-3.

Page 6, **91 per cent:** Deloitte, *2017 Global Mobile Consumer Survey,* 3.

Page 6, **"I can't imagine my life":** International Advertising Bureau UK, *The IAB Future Facing Mobile Study, future facing summary,* www.iabuk.net/system/tdf/research-docs/future%20facing%20summary.pptx?file=1&type=node&id=20133

Page 6, **during sex:** Dominique Mosbergen, "More Than 60 Percent of British Women Check Their Phones During Sex: Survey", 24 July 2013, http://www.huffingtonpost.co.uk/entry/phones-during-sex-british-survey_n_3640820

Page 11, **heavy use of smartphones:** Jose De-Sola Gutiérrez et al., "Cell-Phone Addiction: A Review," *Frontiers in Psychiatry* 7 (October 2016), www.ncbi.nlm.nih.gov/pmc/articles/PMC5076301.

Page 11, **"it's not an exaggeration":** Jean M. Twenge, "Have Smartphones Destroyed a Generation?" *The Atlantic,* 3 August 2017, Technology, www.theatlantic.com/amp/article/534198.

Page 12, **otherwise mentally healthy people:** Adam Gazzaley and Larry D. Rosen, *The Distracted Mind: Ancient Brains in a High-Tech World* (Cambridge:

MIT Press, 2016), 152–57, and Larry D. Rosen, *iDisorder: Understanding Our Obsession with Technology and Overcoming Its Hold on Us* (New York: St. Martin's Griffin, 2012).

Page 18, **a revolutionary product:** Steve Jobs, "Keynote Address," Macworld 2007, 9 January 2007, Moscone Convention Center, San Francisco, transcript, accessed 13 August 2017, thenextweb.com/apple/2015/09/09/genius-annotated-with-genius.

Page 20, **Whenever you check:** Mark Anthony Green, "Aziz Ansari on Quitting the Internet, Loneliness, and Season 3 of *Master of None*," *GQ*, 2 August 2017, www.gq.com/story/aziz-ansari-gq-style-cover-story.

Page 21, **"Your telephone in the 1970s":** *60 Minutes*, season 49, episode 29, "What Is 'Brain Hacking'? Tech Insiders on Why You Should Care," produced by Guy Campanile and Andrew Bast, reported by Anderson Cooper, aired 11 June 2017, on CBS, www.cbsnews.com/news/what-is-brain-hacking-tech-insiders-on-why-you-should-care.

Page 21, **"They haven't used it":** Nick Bilton, "Steve Jobs Was a Low-Tech Parent," Disruptions, *New York Times*, 11 September 2014, www.nytimes.com/2014/09/11/fashion/steve-jobs-apple-was-a-low-tech-parent.html.

Page 21, **Bill Gates:** Emily Retter, "Billionaire tech mogul Bill Gates reveals he banned his children from mobile phones until they turned 14," *Mirror*, 21 April 2017, Technology, www.mirror.co.uk/tech/billionaire-tech-mogul-bill-gates-10265298.

Page 22, **we can get addicted to behaviours:** In 2014, the *Diagnostic and Statistical Manual of Mental Disorders (DSM-5)* officially included gambling disorders in the list of disorders that can qualify as addictions – the first time a non-substance-related disorder had been classified in this way, and the first time a so-called *behavioural* addiction had been recognised as such.

Page 22, **Norman Doidge explains:** Norman Doidge, *The Brain That Changes Itself: Stories of Personal Triumph from the Frontiers of Brain Science* (New York: Penguin Books, 2007), 106.

Page 22, **a 2015 Consumer Insights report:** Microsoft Canada, *Attention Spans*, Consumer Insights (spring 2015), www.scribd.com/document/31744 2018/microsoft-attention-spans-research-report-pdf.

Page 24, **Just as drugs:** Adam Alter, *Irresistible: The Rise of Addictive Technology and the Business of Getting Us Hooked* (New York: Penguin Press, 2017), 67.

Page 27, **the App Store initially refused:** *60 Minutes*, "What Is 'Brain Hacking'?"

Page 28, **Never before in history:** Bianca Bosker, "The Binge Breaker: Tristan Harris believes Silicon Valley is addicting us to our phones. He's determined to make it stop," *The Atlantic*, November 2016, Technology, www.theatlantic.com/magazine/archive/2016/11/the-binge-breaker/501122.

Page 31, **"we're playing a slot machine":** Tristan Harris, "How Technology Is Hijacking Your Mind – from a Magician and Google Design Ethicist," *Thrive Global*, 18 May 2016, journal.thriveglobal.com/how-technology-hijacks-peoples-minds-from-a-magician-and-google-s-design-ethicist-56d62ef5edf3.

Page 32, **According to Larry Rosen:** Rosen, *iDisorder.*

Page 34, **Adam Alter describes the launch:** Alter, *Irresistible*, 127–28.

Page 34, **associated with depression:** Gazzaley and Rosen, *The Distracted Mind*, 154–56.

Page 34, **at least one lawsuit:** Christopher Coble, "Is Apple Liable for Distracted Driving Accidents?" *FindLaw* (blog), 21 October 2016, blogs.findlaw.com/injured/2016/10/is-apple-liable-for-distracted-driving-accidents.html. See also Matt Richtel, "Phone Makers Could Cut Off Drivers. So Why Don't They?" *New York Times*, 24 September 2016, Technology, www.nytimes.com/2016/09/25/technology/phone-makers-could-cut-off-drivers-so-why-dont-they.html.

Page 36, **"The closer we pay attention":** Harris, "How Technology Is Hijacking Your Mind."

Page 37, **a two-part study:** Timothy D. Wilson et al., "Just Think: The Challenges of the Disengaged Mind," *Science* 345, no. 6192 (4 July 2014), Social Psychology, wjh-www.harvard.edu/~dtg/WILSON%20ET%20AL%202014.pdf.

Page 39, **Facebook is in the surveillance business:** John Lanchester, "You Are the Product," *London Review of Books* 39, no. 16 (17 August 2017): 3–10, www.lrb.co.uk/v39/n16/john-lanchester/you-are-the-product.

Page 40, **Ramsay Brown:** *60 Minutes*, "What Is 'Brain Hacking'?"

Page 40, **the prize these advertisers are after:** Tim Wu, *The Attention Merchants: The Epic Scramble to Get Inside Our Heads* (New York: Vintage Books, 2016).

Page 40, **"the currency of the attention economy":** Ibid.

Page 41, **$31 billion:** Evan LePage, "All the Social Media Advertising Stats You Need to Know," *Social* (blog), Hootsuite, 29 November 2016, blog.hootsuite.com/social-media-advertising-stats; and "U.S. Social Media Marketing–Statistics & Facts," Statista, The Statistics Portal, www.statista.com/topics/1538/social-media-marketing.

Page 41, **39,757 years' worth:** Nick Bilton, "Reclaiming Our (Real) Lives from Social Media," Disruptions, *New York Times*, 16 July 2014, www.nytimes.com/2014/07/17/fashion/reclaiming-our-real-lives-from-social-media.html?mcubz=1. Reporter Nick Bilton based his calculations on data from Facebook itself saying that the average user (in 2014) was spending seventeen minutes per day on the site.

Page 42, **install a Facebook demetricator:** "Facebook Demetricator," Benjamin Grosser, bengrosser.com/projects/facebook-demetricator.

Page 43, **in 2017:** Holly B. Shakya and Nicholas A. Christakis, "Association of Facebook Use with Compromised Well-Being: A Longitudinal Study," *American Journal of Epidemiology* 185, no. 3 (1 February 2017): 203–211, doi. org/10.1093/aje/kww189.

Page 43, *Harvard Business Review:* Holly B. Shakya and Nicholas A. Christakis, "A New, More Rigorous Study Confirms: The More You Use Facebook, the Worse You Feel," *Harvard Business Review*, 10 April 2017, Health, hbr.org/2017/04/a-new-more-rigorous-study-confirms-the-more-you-use-facebook-the-worse-you-feel.

Page 43, **in** *The Atlantic***:** Twenge, "Have Smartphones Destroyed a Generation?"

Page 45, **his memoir,** *Chaos Monkeys:* Antonio García Martínez, *Chaos Monkeys: Obscene Fortune and Random Failure in Silicon Valley* (New York: HarperCollins, 2016), 382.

Page 45, **"biggest accumulation of personal data since DNA":** Ibid., 320.

Page 45, **countless details about your** *offline* **life:** Ibid., 381–82.

Page 47, **The mind cannot:** Sunim, Haemin, *The Things You Can See Only When You Slow Down: How to Be Calm and Mindful in a Fast-Paced World* (New York: Penguin Books, 2017), 65.

Page 48, **twenty-five minutes:** Gazzaley and Rosen, *The Distracted Mind*, 133.

Page 48, **Stanford researchers:** Eyal Ophir, Clifford Nass, and Anthony D. Wagner, "Cognitive Control in Media Multitaskers," *Proceedings of the National Academy of Sciences of the United States of America* 106, no. 37 (15 September 2009): 15583–87, www.pnas.org/content/106/37/15583.full.pdf.

Page 49, **the researchers were wrong:** *Digital Nation*, Interview with Clifford Nass, aired on 1 December 2009, on PBS, www.pbs.org/wgbh/pages/frontline/digitalnation/interviews/nass.html.

Page 50, **Just as neurons:** Nicholas Carr, *The Shallows: What the Internet Is Doing to Our Brains* (New York: W. W. Norton, 2011), 120.

Page 51, **London cab drivers' brains:** Eleanor A. Maguire et. al., "Navigation-related Structural Change in the Hippocampi of Taxi Drivers," *Proceedings of the National Academy of Sciences of the United States of America* 97, no. 8 (10 November 1999): 4398–4403, www.pnas.org/content/97/8/4398.short.

Page 52, **people in the UK were spending:** "Smartphone Use Headed for a New Milestone in the UK", www.emarketer.com/Article/Smartphone-Use-Headed-New-Milestone-UK/1016444

Page 53, **it is** *particularly* **good at doing so:** Carr, *The Shallows*, 115.

Page 54, **Multi-screening trains consumers:** Microsoft Canada, *Attention Spans.*

Page 57, **our brains must make a split-second decision:** Carr, *The Shallows*, 122.

Page 59, **a recipe not for memory:** "Plato on Writing," www.umich.edu/~lsarth/filecabinet/PlatoOnWriting.html. Interestingly, Plato (paraphrasing Socrates) was writing about the written word. Socrates was – rightfully – concerned that the development of written language would affect people's ability to memorise information, since memory had, up until that point, been the only way to record it.

Page 61, **The Magical Number Seven:** George A. Miller, "The Magical Number Seven, Plus or Minus Two: Some Limits on Our Capacity for Processing Information," *The Psychological Review* 63 (1956): 81–97, www.musanim.com/miller1956.

Page 61, **closer to two to four:** Carr, *The Shallows*, 124.

Page 64, **people mistake excitement:** Sayadaw U Pandita, *In This Very Life: The Liberation Teachings of the Buddha* (Somerville, MA: Wisdom Publications, 1992).

Page 65, **Screen time . . . in the hour before bedtime:** Gazzaley and Rosen, *The Distracted Mind*, 139.

Page 66, **the health consequences of chronic fatigue:** Division of Sleep Medicine, "Consequences of Insufficient Sleep," Harvard Medical School, healthysleep.med.harvard.edu/healthy/matters/consequences.

Page 66, **even short-term sleep deprivation:** Ibid.

Page 66, **your brain has difficulty:** Gazzaley and Rosen, *The Distracted Mind*, 93.

Page 66, **the same level of impairment:** Division of Sleep Medicine, "Judgment and Safety," Harvard Medical School, last modified 16 December 2008, healthysleep.med.harvard.edu/need-sleep/whats-in-it-for-you/judgment-safety#6.

Page 67, **"Sleep deprivation can affect memory":** Gazzaley and Rosen, *The Distracted Mind*, 94.

Page 68, **"I have to raise my imagination game":** Michael Hainey, "Lin-Manuel Miranda Thinks the Key to Parenting Is a Little Less Parenting," *GQ*, 26 April 2016, Entertainment, www.gq.com/story/unexpected-lin-manuel-miranda.

Page 69, **We learn to stay:** Pema Chodron, "The Shenpa Syndrome," *Awakin. org*, 14 March 2005, www.awakin.org/read/view.php?tid=385.

Page 70, **"Mindfulness is about seeing the world:** Judson Brewer, *The Craving Mind: From Cigarettes to Smartphones to Love – Why We Get Hooked & How We Can Break Bad Habits* (New Haven: Yale University Press, 2017), 13.

Page 71, **Brewer and his colleagues:** J. A. Brewer et al., "Mindfulness Training for Smoking Cessation: Results from a Randomized Controlled Trial," *Drug and Alcohol Dependence* 119, nos. 1–2 (2011): 72–80.

Page 72, **"She moved from wisdom":** Brewer, *The Craving Mind*, 29–30.

Page 74. **"[W]e must act":** Tim Wu, *The Attention Merchants: The Epic Scramble to Get Inside Our Heads* (New York: Vintage, 2016), 353.

Page 76, **Everyone knows:** William James, *Principles of Psychology* (New York: Dover, 1890), 403-4.

Page 88, **"phone meditation" exercise:** James Bullen, "How to Better Manage Your Relationship with Your Phone," ABC Health & Wellbeing, 11 August 2017, www.abc.net.au/news/health/2017-08-12/how-to-better-manage-your-relationship-with-your-phone/8784384.

Page 96, **much more effective than saying:** Alter, *Irresistible*, 272.

Page 100, **exercise that increases blood flow:** Gazzaley and Rosen, *The Distracted Mind*, 203–5, 209.

Page 102, **"slaves are fully aware":** Nassim Nicholas Taleb, "Stretch of the Imagination," *NewStatesman*, Observations, 2 December 2010, www.new statesman.com/ideas/2010/11/box-procrustes-call-bed-taleb.

Page 103, **a 2008 study:** Anna Rose Childress et al., "Prelude to Passion: Limbic Activation by 'Unseen' Drug and Sexual Cues," *PLoS ONE* 3, no. 1 (30 January 2008): e1506, doi.org/10.1371/journal.pone.0001506.

Page 105, **the mere presence of a smartphone on the table:** Shalini Misra et al., "The iPhone Effect: The Quality of In-Person Social Interactions in the Presence of Mobile Devices," *The Sage Journal of Environment and Behavior* 48, issue 2 (1 July 2014), journals.sagepub.com/doi/abs/10.1177/0013916514 539755.

Page 105, **make us hallucinate:** Daniel J. Kruger, "What's Behind Phantom Cell Phone Buzzes?" *The Conversation*, 16 March 2017, theconversation.com/whats-behind-phantom-cellphone bunes 73029.

Page 105, **an average of 14.7 times:** Caitlin O'Connell, "2015: The Year That Push Notifications Grew Up," *Localytics* (blog), 10 December 2015, info. localytics.com/blog/2015-the-year-that-push-notifications-grew-up.

Page 128, **in one information patch:** Gazzaley and Rosen, *The Distracted Mind*, 179.

Page 130, **we will always be speeding:** Pema Chödrön, *When Things Fall Apart: Heart Advice for Difficult Times* (Boston: Shambhala Publications, 1997), 34.

Page 132, **physical changes to the brain:** Carr, *The Shallows*, 51.

Page 133, **As Maryanne Wolf writes:** Maryanne Wolf, *Proust and the Squid: The Story and Science of the Reading Brain* (New York: Harper Perennial, 2007), 217–18.

Page 134, **"ignoring is an active process":** Gazzaley and Rosen, *The Distracted Mind*, 55, 56.

Page 134, **good for our working and long-term memories:** Ibid., 66–68.

Page 134, **a secularised form:** Ibid., 190, 231, and Brewer, *The Craving Mind*, 167, 175.

Page 140, **"maximising":** Barry Schwartz, *The Paradox of Choice: Why More Is Less* (New York: Ecco Press, 2016).

Page 142, **Have a Fleeting Relationship:** Calvin Morrill, David Snow, and Cindy White, eds. *Together Alone: Personal Relationships in Public Spaces* (Berkeley: University of California Press, 2005) and Vanessa Gregory, "The Fleeting Relationship," *New York Times Magazine*, 11 December 2005, www.nytimes.com/2005/12/11/magazine/fleeting-relationship-the.html.

Page 143, **It is easy:** Ralph Waldo Emerson and Stanley Appelbaum, *Self-reliance, and Other Essays* (New York: Dover Publications, 1993).

ABOUT THE AUTHOR

SARA REMINGTON

Catherine Price is an award-winning writer and science journalist whose work has appeared in publications including *The Best American Science Writing*; the *New York Times*, *The Washington Post Magazine*, *Los Angeles Times*, *San Francisco Chronicle*, *Popular Science*, *O: The Oprah Magazine*, *Men's Journal*, *Parade*, *Salon*, *Slate*, and *Outside*, among others. Her previous books include *Vitamania: How Vitamins Revolutionized the Way We Think about Food*; *101 Places Not to See Before You Die*; *Mindfulness: A Journal* and *The Big Sur Bakery Cookbook*. You can learn more about her work (and get in touch with her) at catherine-price.com or howtobreakupwithyourphone.com. She lives in Philadelphia, and her Twitter handle is @catherine_price, but she doesn't check it much.

INDEX